TIMESTUDY FUNDAMENTALS
FOR FOREMEN

BOOKS BY PHIL CARROLL

Timestudy Fundamentals for Foremen

Phil Carroll

with a foreword by **GLENN GARDINER**
*Formerly Vice-President, Forstmann Woolen Company; author of
"Practical Foremanship"*

THIRD EDITION

McGRAW-HILL BOOK COMPANY

New York   St. Louis   San Francisco   Düsseldorf   Johannesburg
Kuala Lumpur   London   Mexico   Montreal   New Delhi
Panama   Rio de Janeiro   Singapore   Sydney   Toronto

Carroll, Phil
  Timestudy fundamentals for foremen.

  Bibliography: p.
  1. Time study. 2. Foremen. I. Title.
T60.4.C37 1972   658.5'421   72-5127
ISBN 0-07-010145-0

1 2 3 4 5 6 7 8 9 0 BPBP 7 6 5 4 3 2

*The editors for this book were W. Hodson Mogan and Lydia Maiorca,
the designer was Naomi Auerbach, and its production was supervised
by Teresa F. Leaden. It was set in Baskerville by Brown Brothers
Linotypers, Inc.*

It was printed and bound by The Book Press.

To
MY DAD, *who said*

*"Always give a little more than they pay for
and you will never have to worry about a job."*

Contents

Foreword

We know some foremen who "pooh-pooh" the whole subject of timestudy, and we suspect that they take this attitude because the subject has usually been treated in such technical terms that it was difficult to understand. Someone has said, "What we do not understand, we ridicule."

The purpose of this book on timestudy, written for foremen, is to give the practical foreman a working knowledge of the elementary principles involved in studying and measuring the time it takes to do a job.

The labor cost of any job is merely the money value in wages of the time it takes a man to perform the job. A useless or unnecessary motion takes time just the same as a necessary motion. If we can reduce motion to the minimum essentials, we, therefore, succeed in getting a job done at lower cost. At the same time we make the job easier and less fatiguing for the operator.

The elimination of waste motions also improves the safety of a job. The fewer the motions required to perform an operation the less exposure to hazard.

But, we can't do an intelligent job of eliminating needless motions unless we correctly measure and study the time required for each detail or element involved in the performance of a job. This is where timestudy comes in.

It has always been a recognized part of every foreman's job to make improvements in methods. Many foremen have risen to higher positions because of the success with which they improved methods on jobs they supervised. It is easy to improve the method on a job where an awkward or wasteful motion "sticks out like a sore thumb." There are thousands of jobs, however, in which the inefficiencies, the waste motions, and the time-wasting operations are not apparent to casual observation or to even fairly close observation. A more detailed measurement of small time elements may be required to detect *where* method improvement should be made and *how* it should be made.

The wise foreman will not spurn the fruits of timestudy. He will regard timestudy as a lever, or a tool, to be used in a never-ending search for opportunities to improve job methods.

It is not the purpose of this book to make timestudy engineers out of foremen. The fundamental purpose is to give foremen readers a clear understanding of the principles of timestudy. Understanding those principles, they will be able to make more practical application of timestudy information available to them. They will be better equipped to utilize to the utmost the available services of timestudy specialists in the organization. They will be better able to sell time standards to the operators whom they supervise.

Much of our industrial future in America depends upon the efficiency of job methods. In the months and years ahead we are certain to find ourselves here in America in keen competition with low-cost labor throughout the world. After the war there will be a rush to capture world markets. If our American standard of living for our industrial employees is to be maintained, our production per man per hour will have to be at the highest level in the entire world. This cannot be accomplished by getting American producers to work harder. It can be accomplished by devising work methods that are free from waste motions so that the same human effort can achieve higher productive results.

Foremen in America can and will play a most important part in maintaining American living standards.

Glenn Gardiner

Preface

Talks with supervisors in some 270 plants have convinced me that foremen need training in timestudy principles. Many have asked questions that showed almost complete lack of understanding.

To inform, a great many companies have used this little book to conduct sessions with supervisors, trainees, and union representatives. One plant got excellent results by exposing every supervisor to an "appreciation course." The works manager was the "teacher" of the first group of department heads, both line and staff. Later, discussions with foremen were conducted by pairs of department heads.

Each session was stimulated by true-false statements set up for the chapter assigned. These provoked discussion because they were designed with loopholes for incomplete thinking. The gaps were brought out by going all around the table with each statement. The purpose was to get the members to "educate" each other. For my money, this method accomplishes much more than any teacher-student arrangement.

These true-false statements have been revised twice and printed for distribution. Further, I have developed a Discussion Leaders' Manual to aid in drawing out "all the angles."

However, the group discussion method does only about half the job, in my opinion. The other half must be done with the individual foreman in his own department. He has numerous specific questions about "his work." You know the usual comment, "My work is different."

Informative sessions of some kind are necessary. All those affected by work measurement, both directly and indirectly, must understand. I believe understanding has to come before acceptance. Therefore, we should try to remove the "mystery." People must know the "whys and wherefores." Otherwise, they get out of step. Then, the plant loses part of the effectiveness of the work measurement plan.

Mr. Foreman must know the answers because timestudy is so widely used with wage incentives. He will increase industrial relations problems if he tries to duck questions that bear on incentive earnings. Besides, timestudy and incentive have tremendous economic advantages. They contribute as no other tool to our standard of living.

Too, the foreman should learn all he can about timestudy for personal reasons. Its principles can help him to see the truths of many fundamentals of good business. The author believes this so strongly that he suggests every prospective foreman be given at least two years of intensive training in timestudy.

Some beginners and students may find this brief explanation helpful. It leaves out much of a technical nature in order to avoid confusion. On the other hand, trained timestudy men will find great gaps here. They may use "Timestudy for Cost Control" as a follow-up.

To bring the book to this third edition, I acknowledge the gracious help given me by numerous foremen and supervisors. In addition, I wish to thank the managers of many plants for the opportunities afforded me to learn about timestudy. Appreciation is extended also to the friendly critics of my previous efforts to explain timestudy. Again, I solicit criticisms of any who read this edition.

Further, we are indebted to Harold Carter for the "road map" portraying the timestudy steps and to S. J. Kubek for drawing the personalized one. The third was stolen from Jack Barnacal and extended by my daughter Pat. Appreciation is expressed to Gil Young, George Logie, Carl Roll, Gus Young, and Al Stanek who pointed out defects and kept endless scores for the true-false revisions. The suggestions for improvements were completed by Fred Hornbruch, George McRae, Munroe Stiner, Roy Bailey, Earle Miller, and Charlie Thomas.

We are indebted to Ralph Presgrave for permission to include three cartoons drawn by Guy Rutter for Woods & Gordon, Toronto. These are important additions to those originally drawn for articles published in Manufacturing and Industrial Engineering by C. Aubrey C. Grey, Editor.

In the actual preparation, Charlie Thomas, Betty Celler, Atlee O'Brien, and Patricia Edwards did the work for which I take all the credit. Revising a book is a real chore. You should try it sometime. You might find it more difficult than writing a new one. So give my helpers a "big hand."

Phil Carroll

TIMESTUDY FUNDAMENTALS
FOR FOREMEN

CHAPTER ONE

What Timestudy
Gives to Industry

We Americans enjoy the highest standard of living in the world. We have better food, clothes, and homes. We own more radios, automobiles, and bathtubs. That is because we have to spend fewer hours of labor to buy the products we want. But this didn't just happen. It was caused by what we call higher productivity.

In shop language, productivity is the rate of turning out production. You may think of it as "pieces per hour." Americans turn out more production per hour, and that is why we have so much more of the "good things" of life.

Timestudy Foundation

High productivity results from timestudy. Why this is true may cause you to wonder. You may say, "I never heard of timestudy before." But stop and think.

Haven't you ever said to your boss something like, "It takes me 25 minutes to get to work." Chances are you tried out several ways to get the time down to 25 minutes. You were making a study of time when you figured out shortcuts to your plant so that you could sleep longer in the mornings.

"That ain't timestudy," you may reply. But what you mean is that you didn't use a "stopwatch." Thus, all we're talking about is the smallness of watch readings.

Easier Ways

Whether you use the wall clock, your wristwatch, or no timing device at all, you are making a study of time whenever you think up a better way. You may work out some gadget to help shorten the time. You may get a better machine. Such improvements increase productivity. They add to the output per man-hour. That is how we have made America great.

Industrial Progress

All of us want better goods at lower prices. To get them, the only way I know that is legal is through more efficient production. That is a vital reason why you are interested in timestudy. And your men are interested too. They want more of the "comforts of life."

The comforts we now have were luxuries not so very long ago. I can remember reading by coal-oil lamps and going outdoors to pump drinking water. This is not a book on history. But recognize the progress we have made.

The more we want we can have only when we produce more during our work time. This is a very important fundamental to keep in mind. Already we are losing ground in our struggles with competition from abroad.

Getting Facts

What we need are more facts concerning the ways we now use our *time*. The study of "time taken" is the starting point of many improvements that can be made in industry. Such studies will reveal ways to save time or to improve its use. Hence, timestudy is a practical way to get facts about any production process. The basic facts are the small time elements recorded on the timestudies. Along with these are noted the uses made of the time. Analysis, investigation, and the repeated question "Why?" turn these facts into practical uses. The facts are in time, and time is the basis of industrial operations. The time facts are most useful to you in your progressive efforts to produce more with the men and machines you now have. Thus, timestudies are valuable to you if they serve no other useful purpose than supplying you with time facts.

Timestudy Basis

Timestudy is a comparatively new tool—it is only about 80 years old. It was started primarily because more output had to be produced with the men and machines available. Its use has continued because it is the best method we have for studying time taken to do work.

Timestudy is used like a sieve to sort useful work from lost time and wasted effort. As a by-product, the elements of useful work are added together to establish work standards. These serve many purposes. Primarily, by comparison, standards aid in revealing reoccurrences of extra work and waiting time.

Output Measurement

Another important use of work standards is the measurement
of individual output. The quantity produced per unit of time
is one measure of applied skill. Time must be considered because there are very few jobs where even the most highly
skilled person could support himself unless he put his abilities
to work often enough. Skill must be applied diligently to have

Fig. 1-1. Measures of skill and ability are very important to each of us as
individuals.

commercial value. In industry, that application is measured in time taken to produce products.

Such measures of output are looked upon favorably by most people. They like to know how well they are performing. And usually, they holler loudly when delays and extra work interfere with their production. Notice Figure 1-1.

Employee Training

Too, work measures are very helpful when you are training men. Both you and your men can gauge the progress being made. Besides, you can reduce the training period. You can use the details listed on the timestudies as aids. These show the sequence of elements in the operation. With this breakdown, you can much more easily explain just exactly how an operation is to be done. A complete and correct explanation is of great value when you are instructing anyone in a method to be used.

Employee Progress

You may feel that new employees should not be placed on standard. From certain points of view, you are correct. On the other hand, without measuring the production of good pieces turned out

1. How can you know if the new or transferred employee is progressing satisfactorily?
2. How can you tell when the new employee has been fully trained and is competent?
3. How will you learn that the new employee is not suited to the work he is being trained to do?

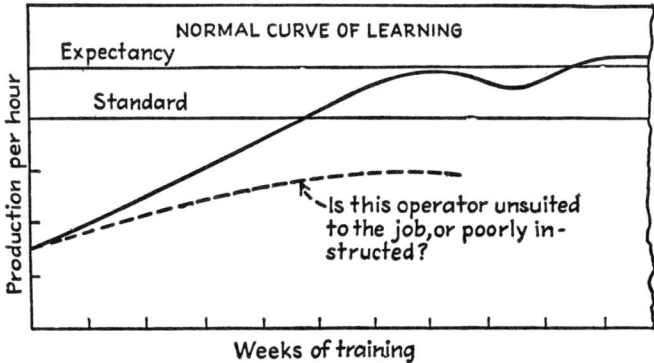

Fig. 1-2. If the operator's skill does not improve as rapidly as you expect, the fault may lie with either incomplete instruction or improper placement.

These and other questions can be answered by measuring the production of the trainee. Study the "learning curve" shown in Figure 1-2. With figures to guide, you can tell whether the new man is making progress as rapidly as he should. You may discover much earlier that the new or transferred man would be better suited to some other kind of work.

Increasing Productivity

The efforts made by individuals to show good performances result in better productivity. In turn, this calls for a higher caliber of foremanship.

1. You will be requested to reduce occurrences of extra work that slow down production.
2. You will be urged by your people to reduce the amount of delay time that prevents working.
3. You will be prompted to get all jobs measured by work standards. See Figure 1-3.

Fig. 1-3. "Aw, give me another job. This one is daywork."

As you improve the managing of your department, productivity will increase further. You will be getting salable output in place of the higher costs of lost time and extra work.

Improving Methods

As you study the times now taken, you are sure to see ways to improve upon your present methods. Many operations in every department can be bettered. Probably too, when you show more interest in finding better methods, your men will suggest some improvements. They may tell you about the unnecessary walking and reaching they have to do. Such comments may prompt you to rearrange the layout of your department. You may need to change some equipment locations in order to reduce unbalanced work loads.

No doubt you will notice some work being done that is wasted effort. For example, you may be putting a fine finish all over some piece that needs to be finished on only one surface. When you see an operation like that, ask yourself, "Would I pay a higher price to get white enamel on the back of my refrigerator?" "Certainly not," you say. "It goes against the wall."

How many operations just as useless do you have in your department? How much time is being spent that you can convert into useful production? Remember, somebody has to pay for added operations and waiting time. If these added costs make your company's prices too high, you will lose the jobs.

Enlarging Capacity

All such gains you make cut into a cost you may not think of. To emphasize, it costs $44,000 to provide one work place in a plant I know. Considering such expenses, most of the foremen I know are not privileged to write out a requisition for

　　1　　2A Warner & Swasey
　　　　　　　　or
　　1　　1600# Hermann Rollover

Usually, they have to get the "approval of Congress" to get more or different equipment. In contrast, you can avoid such requests by utilizing the time analyses made by timestudy. All the improvements you make in man performances, time savings, and work methods will add to your department's capacity. The betterments increase your production per man-hour. Such gains are beneficial. In effect, these improvements produce the same results as more men, more machines, and larger plants.

And if your output goes up, you have reduced overhead cost per unit. That means your company is in a better position to keep going longer.

Better Planning

To get the most from these gains, better planning and scheduling are necessary. Otherwise, people who work more effectively will wait longer. They will run out of work. Note Figure 1-4. In planning, work standards are a great help. They give you two factors needed for reliable scheduling. These are

1. Time standards that indicate process times
2. Employee performances that measure actual productivities.

Fig. 1-4. You cannot solve delivery problems unless you improve your planning. The stock-chaser method sets back all jobs.

You must have both to make a plan workable. The plan by itself is not worth much without consistent performances. It is the more uniform rate of production that makes a work schedule more practical. A good schedule is helpful to you. It gets work to your people so you can avoid "down time." But also, it pushes you to plan ahead for tools, drawings, and instructions.

Better Deliveries

Nearly all improvements bring about a reduction in process time. The result is that work can be turned out more quickly. Consequently, you can make better deliveries to your company's customers. That is important because much of your company's business depends upon the ability to make better deliveries than your competitors. Therefore, the quicker the delivery, the better the opportunity for your company to get more business.

Besides, faster deliveries give you a personal advantage. They reduce your inventory. To see this, take a look at the diagram in Figure 1-5. This portrays the usual lot or batch type of operation. People pick up pieces, perform operations, and put back the items in a tote pan or truck. Then the parts are carted to the next operation. There they sit. They add to inventory.

You can shrink both the work time and the sit time. The benefits are dual. See Figure 1-6. Your company's deliveries are improved and your inventory is reduced.

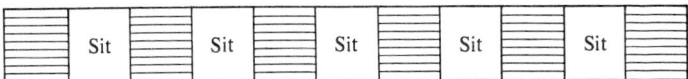

Fig. 1-5. Batch or lot operation cycles are made up of work time and sit time.

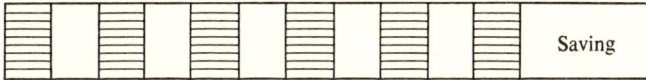

Fig. 1-6. You can improve delivery and cut inventory by shrinking both work time and sit time.

Attaining Estimates

Before delivery becomes urgent, "What price?" is the question. Often a price is set by estimate. Such estimates are quite reliable when Manufacturing and Timestudy get together to agree upon methods and times. Such prior planning is potent for its effect upon the success of the business. The company must make money. Otherwise, it will "go broke" and no employee will have his job.

However, note carefully. Two factors enter into the reliability of guesstimates. One is the correctness of the standards used. The other, which you control, is the performances on standards and the interferences with them.

Cost Standards

Of course, if you can estimate prices, you can set cost standards. Those for labor are the products of established wage rates and standard times. Certainly, standard costs of parts and assemblies must contain material items and overhead. Also, the cost of material must take into account reasonable allowances for defectives and scrap.

Labor is usually the major variable. On daywork, the labor cost varies "all over the map." The reasons are many:

1. The work time includes all kinds of uncontrolled delays and added work.
2. The methods are whatever the man himself devises.

3. The attitude is, "There's nothing in it for me" to get the job done.

In contrast, with standard times, the labor costs of the operations are practically uniform. Small variations occur. Different hourly rates, delay times, and extra operations increase costs. But the variations are very much less than under daywork. This helps you. The reason is that one of your prime responsibilities is the control of costs. With standards, you can do this much better. With timestudy, you have the means for reducing those costs.

Wage Incentive

All the advantages cited for work measurement are increased when standards are used with wage incentive. Modern incentive plans are based on good timestudy. And remember, we had wage incentive before we had the Bible.

Incentive is important for two reasons. First, it adds to the earning capacities of those who work on it. Second, it helps to further reduce the costs of the things we buy. Costs are lower and more uniform. Those are good reasons why the two-way advantage of incentive is so widely used in progressive plants today. Either of the two results just mentioned is very worthwhile. When both are gained, the benefits are multiplied in what we know as *real wages*. Additions to real wages are quite different from pay raises. Too often, wage increases are followed by price inflation.

Higher Earnings

Do you realize that a good wage incentive plan provides the opportunity for increasing earnings about 25 percent? That is more than two 10 percent raises in pay. But wage increases raise costs—not lower them.

More than the 25 percent usually stated can be earned by those with exceptional energy or skill. Such increases are open to those who are interested in getting ahead. It is assumed, of course, that neither management nor union is foolish enough to set "top limits" on incentive earnings.

On the other hand, beginners and those who are not willing to work will not be able to earn the expected amounts of premium. They may say that the "system" is at fault. However, it must be clearly understood that an incentive plan provides only the *opportunity* to increase earnings. It cannot carry a guarantee of any stated percent of premium and still be an incentive plan. Any such guarantee of premium is a disguised wage increase.

Individual Opportunity

The opportunity to increase earnings is usually set up on an individual basis. Consequently, the man himself can very frequently "write his own ticket." What he earns depends upon his skills and how diligently he applies them. He must work at an above normal pace to earn extra money.

People working individually usually produce more than if they were in groups. For that reason, many companies avoid the use of "group" payment wherever possible. Group incentive has its good points, of course. But it is not used where the disadvantages of averaging the premium earnings of individual operators are fully considered. Nor is it used where it seems important to measure individual skill and ability.

With individual incentive, the skilled man has the opportunity to compare his performance with others having similar

EMPLOYEE	WEEK ENDING FEB 7						WEEK ENDING F				
	M	T	W	T	F	S	M	T	W	T	F
JOHN SMITH	72	75	69	80	76	79	65	72	76	75	
ROBERT JONES	65	68	70	69	71	65	68	72	73	69	
RUFUS BLACK	75	78	82	83	79	73	71	76	80	82	
WILLIAM REIS	61	63	66	61	64	62	63	69	71	65	
JOSEPH McKEE	N	E	W	58	64	70	55	61	64		
JACOB TAYLOR	N	E	W	36	47	45	51	49	58		
RALPH THOMPSON	N	E	W		36	38	35	41	44		
EDWARD BURNS	81	83	86	84	81	73	78	82	85	84	

Fig. 1-7. Many shops post performances daily. Figures shown here are in terms of 60 units per hour as normal.

skills. Note the chart in Figure 1-7. The highly skilled individual can be paid according to his production. Sound wage incentive is the fairest method we have for rewarding unusual skill and ability.

Quality Production

Obviously, quality must be maintained in the operation of an incentive plan. If not, the company may lose its customers. Besides, any standards for wage incentive must be based upon some definitions of acceptable quality. Of course, some will argue that more time will permit the producer to do a better job. But there is a practical limit to that. There is a reasonable time established by commercial prices. Prices are set by what customers are willing to pay. It is here that quality workmanship turned out in reasonable time becomes important in competitive business conduct.

Quality Workmanship

What we have just stated about quality raises the question concerning the effects of incentive. Some think that quality suffers when incentive is used. Actually, the opposite is true. To be sure, there may be more pieces spoiled per day. That can happen with any increase in production. The correct answer lies in the ratio of total poor to total good pieces. This ratio should go down under good incentive operation. The reason is simple. The producer has a better job to hang on to. For example, a $2.80 an hour employee often becomes at least a $3.50 wage earner.

Naturally, you and the other supervisors must be strong enough to hold quality to the same standards that were met prior to the installation of incentive. You dare not try, as some do, to substitute wage incentive for better managing. When you really "run your department," pride in workmanship is increased. Higher average quality is turned out.

Safer Work

Right here, it might be well to mention safety. The reason for discussing it is to correct a false notion. Certain people think that "daywork" is safer than incentive. Such is not the case. The reason is clear. Men on incentive are alert and busy. They are not half asleep trying to kill time. Their minds are on their jobs. They don't forget to watch what they are doing. They are safer operators, as a rule. Admittedly, some are reckless and greedy. They disregard the safety devices. But this type of employee is a hazard under either condition; that is, if he doesn't kill himself in the automobile, he wraps around a tree.

Promotions Hastened

With standards set for quality and quantity, an individual on incentive has the opportunity to demonstrate what he can do. The results are computed and recorded. Sometimes the performances are posted in the shop. See Figure 1-7. Such records often show good pieces and scrap as well as incentive premiums. The postings of incentive earnings tend to pull the low producer up to the better performers.

That is one of the most helpful advantages of wage incentive that many people fail to recognize. It gives the employees, and others, a comparative measure of applied skills without the influence of opinions. This makes for better industrial relations. It reduces the feeling that "you gotta have pull to get any place around here." Too, it helps the individual to see that he can make his own opportunities for advancement.

CHAPTER TWO

Why You Should Understand Timestudy

"My costs can't be cut any further. They are the lowest they have ever been." Is that what you say when your boss asks you to cut costs? If you do, you are making a big mistake. Here's why.

There are a great many supervisors who *could and did* work out better ways to turn out production. That is why the Committee for Economic Development could report, "The great increase in real wages during the last several generations has been made possible only by a large rise in production per man-hour."

Job Security

But there are more compelling reasons. Most important to you perhaps is your desire to eat regularly. You want to keep your job. And I like to believe that you wish to get your boss's position. Neither is possible if your company folds up. It will if competition here and abroad takes away enough of your company's business.

As you know, customers go to the company that delivers the same or better quality at lower prices. Customers are funny people. They are just like you and me. We shop around, don't we? We have many items in mind that we desire to buy with the money we have. But we must stretch our paycheck. Your company and its customers are no different. Both are groups of people with only the money to spend that comes in from their customers. Both must further reduce their costs so as to continue successful operations.

Company Policy

With your strong incentive to survive, you must work within your company policies. When your management has decided to use work measurement, it becomes one of the "rules of the game." Your score is determined, in part, by how well you play on the team. And I'm not talking "politics." Just going along for the ride can ruin you and your company.

Call it "company policy" if you like. Think of it as a "top brass decision" if you prefer. It is a decision made to improve the profit-making possibilities of your company. That decision was made by the officers of your company who are responsible for its success. Are you going to get aboard? Or will you drag your feet?

Your management is made up of men like you and me. Think ahead, you may be the boss-man yourself one of these days. Who knows? I have seen it happen more than once. In that position, you might make the same decision. How would you feel if your supervisors acted as though they thought you didn't know what you were doing?

Intelligent Selfishness

Why not use what James F. Lincoln calls "Intelligent Selfishness"? Why not make "the most of your opportunities"? That is the way to succeed according to Edgar Guest. Why not use all the means you have to ensure your future? You are living in times when competition is becoming more intense.

Men, Materials, Machines

To succeed, you have to turn out the products your customers want, when they want them, at prices they are willing to pay. In doing this job, you combine "men, materials, and machines." But notice that in that common 3M expression there is no mention of *time*. Those three items without *time* would not give you very much output. Looked at the other way around, only people can turn out production. Man-time is what you work with as a supervisor.

How Much Time

Practically, you can argue that the "man" part is meant to include time. But both are needed. In reality, it is the skill your people apply during work time that counts. Naturally, the degree of skill alters the time required to do a job. Thus, the length of time becomes the chief factor in cost and delivery.

Minutes Are Costs

It is just as well that we do not have all the time we want. Time costs money. As a matter of fact, probably time is the largest cost that you must control. Material may cost more. However, as a rule, you can control only the scrap. Therefore, you are selfishly interested in learning how better to control the very large item of "time cost." If time in your department is too far out of line, soon you may be out of business. That can happen. The wide-awake foremen in the plants that compete with yours are busily studying ways to reduce their costs.

Foreman Training

Important as *time* is, some foremen do not know how to make the best use of it. Their training courses stress cost, production, and industrial relations. These subjects are important. But not enough is said about time. Yet, if you properly take care of the time of your people, you will get the results you are held responsible for.

Understanding Timestudy

To do a better job, you should understand more thoroughly how to study time. It is the foundation of what is sometimes called *scientific management*. This is a "highfalutin' " name for progressive management. And you, personally, want to keep ahead of the parade. For that reason, you want to know the best ways to solve your cost and production problems.

More knowledge of timestudy can be the biggest help to you. To make the most use of it, you should become as much of an expert with timestudy as you are with the other tools you use. Timestudy is thoroughly practical. You can use it every day. It will point out the lost time and wasted effort in your department.

Time Factors

To get started, you must know there are two kinds of time. These are *standard time* and *actual time* Next, you should understand that the term "standard" is used in two ways. These are explained by the following statements:

Standard is the base time allowance for a defined amount of work to be done to standard quality.

Standard time is the total allowed time computed by multiplying good pieces finished by operation *standards*.

Standard time is the measure of output. To determine rate of output—productivity—efficiency—you compare the standard time with the actual time taken to produce it.

Time taken is the net actual time worked to turn out the production being measured.

Such comparisons may be made for one piece, for a lot of parts, or for the day's work. Notice, however, that the statement about "time taken" includes the restriction "net." This means credit must be given for delays. Hence, to improve productivity, you must control lost time.

Reducing Waste

Lost time is not like spoiled material. Scrap can be melted and reprocessed. But time that has been wasted is gone forever. And yet, wasted time can be seen in many operations that are carried on every day.

Time is wasted when people stand around waiting for something to do. Observe the time being lost in Figure 2-1. If a foreman had to wait for a bus as long as he permits some of his operators to wait for their next jobs, he would be "sore." Perhaps he does not notice the time his men wait because he is busy checking his cost reports.

Fig. 2-1. When you hold a conference with a fellow supervisor or attend a meeting, many of your people may be waiting for work.

Time Taken

Between "waits" is the time taken to do the work. This is like the *low-cost* part of our living expenses. What we have left as savings is greater when our living costs come down. In the same way, productivity is increased when the time taken is lowered. It is here that you can be so helpful. You can reduce lost time. You can train your people to be highly skillful. You can teach the right methods and explain the "whys and wherefores" of work measurement.

Training Men

Probably, you know the importance of teaching the correct methods to your people. Unless you train them, you cannot expect them to become high producers. Your men may be trying but not succeeding because you have not fully taught them the proper methods. Again, they may not be meeting standards because they are not putting forth the proper efforts.

You know full well that it takes longer to do a job the wrong way. Therefore, you are handicapping your people if you fail to teach them the proper methods of working. Here again, a knowledge of timestudy will help you to decide that your first act is not to cry, "The standard is too tight." It may be. But the chances are that something else is wrong. Frequently, the fault lies with you as a supervisor. Remember, your job includes teaching as well as leadership. You must do both—train people and inspire effort.

Your Responsibility

To be a real representative of management, you must assume all your responsibilities. Certainly, your jobs are to get out production and to look after your people. Still, with work standards, you have another major duty. As a good manager, you must know when working conditions are not as they should be for the proper operation of your department. If the conditions are not normal, the time standards do not apply. You can make standards unfair by tolerating poor

Methods	Supply
Material	Quality
Setup	Timekeeping

Only when all these influencing factors are correct do the standards measure your operations.

When roadblocks show up, you should overcome them. When you cannot do so, you should notify the Timestudy Department. The standard setter should make allowances for extra work that is necessary. Fairness requires that extra time be allowed for required extra work. But keep in mind, all such allowances raise your costs and lower your production. To bring your costs back into line, you have to remove the causes of the added time.

Changing Conditions

Any changes in conditions may affect standards that have been set. Or changes may require that additional timestudies be made. Usually, these changes are known to you before the timestudy man hears about them. Consequently, you must give the timestudy man a chance to keep standards up to date. You need to work with him because you can directly affect the performances of your people. When poor conditions are present, the productivity drops unless allowances are made. On the other hand, when work is eliminated, the standards become loose.

Be careful. You may be like many foremen. You may be alert to only the big changes. But the little ones will cause you most of your troubles. You see, several little ones you may overlook will add up to become big ones.

Passing the Buck

Some foremen argue that keeping track of method changes is the responsibility of the Timestudy Department. So it is. But timestudy men are human. In many plants they are just as busy trying to keep up with their work as you are with yours. Even if they could do it, timestudy men would have to "police" the entire shop in order to catch just a part of the method changes.

But you and your people know when most of the improvements are introduced. Passing the buck to the Timestudy Department does not solve the problem. You must carry out your responsibility in maintaining correct standards. Moreover, you must know enough about timestudy to realize that failure to maintain consistency between standard time allowed and work done will make your job an increasingly unhappy one as the years go by.

Never forget that cooperation is a two-way act. On one side, the timestudy man must be capable and willing to do his job. Often he is. On the other, you should make dead certain to get timestudy help by calling attention to the changes that affect your time standards.

"Rubber Standards of Quality"

Another factor that has an important bearing on the "correct-ness of standard times" is the definition of quality. That is easy to think of in terms of everyday life. For instance, your wife wants to get the brand of coffee she asks for and pays for when she goes to the supermarket. She does not want to get 80 cent coffee when paying for a 95 cent brand. She has a definite standard of quality she expects to get.

The same is true in manufacturing. The quality desired may be higher or lower than in some other shop. But a definite quality standard should be maintained in your shop. To pro-duce that quality, the timestudy standard should include the work necessary. The time allowed should be fair. However, it becomes "loose" and unfair if the quality of accepted work becomes poorer while the standard time remains unchanged.

The standard may be made "loose" if you will take a poor quality lot because the parts are badly needed. In turn, it is made "tight" if you reject the next batch when you have time to correct the defects. Such "rubber" standards of quality can destroy the confidence of your men. Besides, it can pass along

Fig. 2-2. When you permit "rubber" standards of quality, you may pass along to assembly much extra work.

to assembly a lot of "fittin' and filin'." Look at Figure 2-2. What is worse, it may cost you a customer. If he gets a part that does not fit, he may refuse to buy any more of your basic products.

Points to Remember

A number of the foregoing comments are summarized here as a sort of review.

1. Time is spent for productive operations, but also for indirect work and delays.
2. Delay time can be very largely avoided by supplying the employees with the things they need.
3. Waiting time can be practically eliminated by better planning and having the next jobs ready.

4. Indirect work can be reduced by seeing to it that working conditions are kept up to shop standards.

5. Employees must be instructed to obtain credit for all delay time and necessary extra work.

6. Improvements in methods reduce the times required and the standards should be corrected to conform.

7. Quality should be specified and adhered to in order that the product be correct and the standards fair.

Understanding Incentive

Frequently, time standards are used as the basis for wage incentive. This creates the opportunities for people to increase their earnings. Note Figure 2-3. Further, it helps in our way of

Fig. 2-3. Premium under a good incentive plan means extra earnings for above standard production.

life by paying the individual for what he does. Both these results are greatly assisted by the foremen who understand how best to utilize timestudy. These benefits are obtained in larger amounts as we improve our understandings of the method of operation under the incentive plan.

Experts say that one of the basic characteristics of a good incentive plan is that *it must be understood.* This refers primarily to those who benefit from it. Often, the foremen are included among those working on incentive. When that is the case, the departmental outputs are higher and the costs are lower. Perhaps, if more foremen were on incentive, more people would learn to understand the incentive plan more quickly.

Failure to Explain

Having the foremen understand the incentive plan is only part of the solution. It is not so much the plan itself. Most incentive plans are comparatively simple. It is the failure to explain it to the employees that causes the difficulties. The people who work on incentive must know all the particulars about the plan. These can affect their earnings appreciably.

Preventing Complaints

You may say that the timestudy man should explain to your people how the incentive plan works. Perhaps that is his responsibility. Nevertheless, you are the one to whom your men come with their questions. They may ask you, "What happened to my premium?" They may ask why they did not make as much as they expected to. They may wonder why sometimes the standard time comes out to be less than the actual time taken during the timestudy. They may want to know why all the standards are "tight."

Answer Questions

When your men ask questions about timestudy or incentive, will you be able to answer them? Or will you have to say, "I don't know." Note. Saying you do not know is very much better than guessing, and being wrong. When you guess wrong, everyone is in a "helluva mess."

Why not learn the answers? You don't want to lose prestige. Rather, you want more. Then ask yourself this question, "How can I expect to get the boss's job if I don't understand as simple a subject as our incentive plan?"

It is no excuse to say that the timestudy man failed to explain. Maybe he does not know any better because he, too, was poorly trained. That is not a good reason for letting yourself be held back from making progress. You should make certain that you know all the essentials about timestudy and incentive.

Premium Earnings

The most important thing that you must learn about wage incentive is that all the advantages depend upon increased employee earnings. Higher earnings come from turning out more than the standard output. This is different from a wage increase. That only adds to cost.

The real benefits of an incentive plan begin when people earn "real money." The operators must "get theirs." Premium earnings are the "flywheel" that makes incentive work, and those on incentive are expected to make substantial premiums. Here is the acid test of the success of the incentive plan. Also, it is where the results of good foremanship are measured.

Better Supervision

The several points discussed here bring out the general relation of timestudy to good foremanship. These are pertinent enough to know thoroughly. The attempt will be made to enlarge upon these with many more details in the chapters that follow. However, you will not get much from studying about timestudy unless you begin with the right attitude. You must remember that the timestudy man does not run the manufacturing operations. His job is to set the standards. Even so, he can assist in many ways to make you a bigger success in your job.

But you will not encourage the timestudy man to help you if you always blame him when things go wrong. Sure, he makes mistakes once in a while. That is not a good enough reason for criticizing his standards before you get the facts. Nor should you call Timestudy to make extra allowances for extra work that you should eliminate.

When you learn what you need to know about timestudy, you will move ahead more rapidly. You will make progress because you will do a better job of managing your department. You will get things done because you will not waste time blaming someone else

1. If the methods have been changed
2. If the material is off size or condition
3. If the machine is poorly maintained
4. If the man has to hunt for supplies or tools
5. If the next job is not ready to work on
6. If the operator is not properly instructed
7. If the timekeeping is not correctly done
8. If the man is not putting forth incentive effort
9. If the quality standards are like "rubber"
10. If the person does not have sufficient skill

CHAPTER 3

How to Begin a Timestudy

"Timestudy is a mystery to me. I can't understand how they set those rates we get." You have heard men say some things like that, haven't you? So have I, many times. But what do they mean? Are they using the word timestudy when actually they are talking about "rate setting"?

Quick "Rate Setting"

Maybe they got their experiences in plants where "rates were picked out of a hat." Perhaps the method of setting "rates" was one that could not be clearly explained. Probably they have worked in companies where "rates" were set by

1. "Rate setters" who clocked a few overall times
2. Estimators who "guesstimated" their rates

3. Foremen who relied upon their own experiences

4. Accountants who used past performance records

Too Big a Hurry

All of these ways of setting "rates" I call the "cut and try" method. They have given many people some very bad experiences. Frequently, these shortcut ways of "rate setting" were used to avoid real timestudy. Usually, there was too big a rush to "get going on Monday," as suggested by the sketch in Figure 3-1. The results were that a lot of unnecessary work and delay times were buried in the "rates." Such "rates" proved to

Fig. 3-1. Serious mistakes are made when a company rushes into "rate setting."

be loose as years went by. Earnings got all out of line with actual work done.

"Rate Cutting"

Later on, the loose ones were "cut down." Then, when the employees stepped out to make as much as they did before, further cuts were made. In time, we called this "speed up." Naturally, many men have good reasons for questioning the motives of "rate setters." More than that, people who move from such plants to others carry with them attitudes that are based upon their bad experiences.

Foreman Experience

You may think that "rates" set by foremen are okay. You may contend that your knowledge and experience are superior to the timestudy man's. Let's assume you are right. You may know also what the floor-to-floor times are. But there can be big differences between what has been done and *what should be done.*

Lack of Records

What you may have experienced, heard, or read often deals with the single study routine. By this I mean a "rate" is set from viewing a few cycles of one job. Commonly, these quick looks do not produce recordings of correct element break-downs. Thus, at least two critical facts are missing. One is the inclusion of items of lost time and wasted effort. The other is the lack of clear definitions of work to be done.

Poor Approach

Often, the "rate setter" has made some improvements in method. In a machine shop, he might "jack up" the feed or speed. In some cases, he would achieve more changes than in others. As a consequence, he caused inconsistencies among his "rates."

Such an approach brought on complaints about "selecting the operator" and "timing the best man." By this method, the "rate setter" limited his explanations, if any, to a relatively few people. As a result, he created wrong impressions of the fairness of his "rates."

"Rates" and "Rate Setting"

Before we go on, let me explain specific words. Did you notice the quotation marks around the words "rate" and "rate setter" used earlier? They were put there deliberately. I use those terms to describe work that is *not sound timestudy*. Poor timestudy is not what you want to learn about. Therefore, we will not use these words in discussing correct timestudy.

Timestudy Replaces Guesswork

Happily, the number of plants where they guess at their work standards is decreasing rapidly. Now, timestudy is more generally used to determine time standards. However, the use of timestudy does not solve all the problems. One reason is that there are many varieties of timestudies. Some are exceedingly poor. Yes, there is a lot of "phoney" timestudy being done. And there is still too much "rate setting."

Even when correct timestudies are taken and correct standards established, some inequalities will occur later. This happens because method changes are not followed by revisions in standard times. When this is allowed to occur, standards can get almost as badly out of line as when they are poorly set.

Proper Timestudy

More consistent standards can be set by using the standard data method. Too, when you know more precisely what work is allowed for, you can more easily correct for its changes. Therefore, in this book, we will discuss *how to summarize many timestudies into standard data before any standards are set*. The terms we will use are those that go with the standard data method. The ones you want to learn are

Standard—the base time allowance for a defined amount of work to be done to standard quality

Timestudy—a correctly rated detailed breakdown of an operation into its elements with corresponding watch readings

Timestudy man—a thoroughly trained man who is qualified to build standard data for correct work measurement

Standard data—the tables, curves, and charts built up from many timestudies to predetermine consistent time standards

Steps in Timestudy

To help you see the main differences between "rate setting" and the standard data method, take a look at the chart of steps in Figure 3-2. It gives you the whole picture. On it, you can see the tie-in of the several steps in sound timestudy. Notice the two additional steps of comparing and analyzing.

STEPS IN TIMESTUDY FOR STANDARD DATA

STARTING	Discusses work with foreman
	Explains timestudy to people
	Talks about the operations
OBSERVING	Studies the methods being used
	Judges the skill of performance
	Records all conditions of work
RECORDING	Defines elements performed
	Reads the watch and records
	Notes the rating and circles times
MEASURING	Converts rated times to normals
	Applies needed relax factors
	Sets element standard times
COMPARING	Posts element standard times
	Records job specifications
	Reviews range of work studied
ANALYZING	Determines standards for constants
	Plots curves of variable elements
	Builds charts of standard data
SETTING	Establishes standard methods
	Sets operation standards
	Records the standard times
APPLYING	Explains standards to employees
	Verifies correctness of conditions
	Guides foreman in providing services

Fig. 3-2. These steps include two—Comparing and Analyzing—that are not done in the direct timestudy process.

These are the foremost distinctions. There are other vital exceptions too that you will observe as we go along. Each fundamental will be discussed in turn. At this point, you have a roadmap that shows you the direction we will be taking. Later, you may wish to refer to this chart to help you connect the whole process together.

Human Relations

The standard data method is easy to understand. Besides, the technical part is less than a quarter of the total subject. The bulk of the timestudy man's job is what might be called "sales engineering." Perhaps *human relations* is a more correct term. The main portions of this work take place in the first two steps—starting and observing. Getting along with people is by far the most critical part of timestudy work. The reasons are many. Three should be noted here:

1. The results of timestudy depend upon the employee's interest in good performances.
2. The workman's attitude has a marked effect upon his application of his skill.
3. The timestudy man's method of approach makes for a good or poor attitude toward work measurement.

You know how necessary good human relations are. You must work successfully with people in everything you do. Obviously then, you already know about three quarters of the timestudy job. But you may not understand just how the timestudy man applies the same fundamentals. Hence, a brief explanation will help you to learn why and how he works. You need this knowledge. It will be very useful to you in your own work.

Timestudy Signals Change

At the start, the proper "approach" is critical because timestudy signals change. Changes of some kind almost always follow timestudy observations. And it is not the timestudies but the *changes* that require such careful handling. The prospect of changes may cause resentment because

1. We naturally resist changes. Note Figure 3-3.
2. We want to avoid criticism. Observe Figure 3-4.
3. We think first of job security.
4. We are usually very conservative.

(Drawn by Guy Rutter for J. D. Woods & Gordon Limited, Toronto.)

Fig. 3-3. Many people say that it is human nature to resist change.

(Drawn by Guy Rutter for J. D. Woods & Gordon Limited, Toronto.)

Fig. 3-4. Most of us will go out of our way in attempts to avoid criticism.

5. We are inclined to be lazy.

6. We automatically say, "Can't be done."

Many Changes Occur

Knowing how to get people to make changes is essential in good timestudy. It is very important because several different kinds of changes may take place. Some are major. Some are unimportant. Following are a number of the typical changes.

Jobs	Tools
Skills	Methods
Habits	Effort
Locations	Standards
Machines	

Certain of these changes may involve the rearrangement of the work place. If any require moving to a new location or to a new machine, more persuasion is necessary. People get to thinking that certain bench spaces or machines belong to them. The same is true in the office. People put their names on chairs and wastebaskets. Sometimes the first 15 minutes of each day are spent in trying to find the individual's property after the janitor has gotten it mixed up.

Part of this feeling comes from possessiveness. Part results from pride. In the shop, mechanics frequently hate to give up "their" machines. They have taken good care of them. They have kept them in good working order and know what they will do.

Overcoming Objections

To overcome negative attitudes toward the changes that are to be made, persuasion and good salesmanship are necessary.

Of course, needless changes should be avoided. Naturally, more changes will be made when timestudy is first being introduced. However, as someone said, "Nothing is so permanent as change."

Since changes are part of progress, they will continue long after a department has been standardized. Improvements will be introduced. Many will call for restudies. Probably, some standard times will be reduced. They must be if standards are to be kept fair and consistent.

Timestudy Training

Considering the problems of introducing work standards, the timestudy man should be well trained. He must be taught how to make the proper approach in his timestudy efforts. He should be fully aware of the aid it is in doing a good job. Then too, you are vitally interested in this part of timestudy. It concerns you because of the effect it has upon your people. It is telling from two angles.

1. You should see that the timestudy man does his job properly.
2. You should become more expert in getting people to make changes.

Gaining Confidence

Surely the timestudy man has a "selling" job to do. To do this successfully, first of all he must sell himself. He must be able to sell himself before he can sell timestudy standards. You will note just one of his problems by taking a look at Figure 3-5. The timestudy man can take care of such questions when he has a pleasant personality and approaches his work with a fair

Fig. 3-5. Timestudy men must be trained to establish confidence in their work and to overcome the natural objections to changes.

and open mind. He must gain the confidence of the foreman and the employees. He must establish the fact that all are truly concerned with getting correct standards.

The Right Attitude

In getting good results, the timestudy man must have the right attitude. To begin with, he must believe in people. He must remember that the great majority of people are basically fair. All they expect is a fair measure of their efforts. That may seem to contradict the all too common belief.

Many think that the man in the shop will put one over on the timestudy man whenever he can. Actually the question is, "Do they put it over on him because he is inexperienced in timestudy? Or is it because he does not understand men?" Then there is another twist. How can the timestudy man hope to get the right answers if he expects the employees to try to give him a "hosing"?

Keep in mind that the individual timestudy is only a part of the standard data. For that reason, whatever an operator may elect to do should not affect the standards to be set. Just the same, the employee who tries to "amuse" the timestudy man must later be persuaded.

The timestudy man has to start out with the proper attitude. He must know that only a few people are actually dishonest. The rest are willing to give a fair demonstration of the job when the timestudy man knows how to get their interest. To do this, he must expect that people want to be fair.

Explanations Are Necessary

From the foregoing, it should be apparent that the timestudy man must understand how his work affects others. He must explain what he does and why. He must give satisfactory explanations to remove whatever fear or mystery may be present. He can do so more readily when he takes good timestudies as suggested by Figure 3-6. Certainly, his conduct must be such as to inspire confidence. Without confidence, a pleasant personality can accomplish little.

Fig. 3-6. The timestudy man can explain his standards more readily when he has taken good studies.

Avoid Technical Terms

Even when the timestudy man has the right attitude, he may fail in his job of explaining. If he attempts to explain timestudy as it is described in the average textbook, he will create more confusion than understanding. Shopmen are not interested in the form of the timestudy, the kind of watch and its recordings, and a lot of techniques that have no bearing on the answers. Shopmen want to know "Why." Too many technical terms make an explanation seem like an attempt to dodge the issue.

Common Sense Explanation

Timestudy should be explained as common sense. The object is to remove whatever mysteries may exist.

1. Timestudy principles must be understood before they can be made the most use of.
2. Standards must be fair to employees and company for both to succeed in the long run.
3. Extra work and delays not allowed for separately unjustly restrict the employee's performance.
4. Production restricted to cover up loose standards may cause the company to go broke.

Don't Rush

Explanations should be given in small "doses." This method is second nature to the foreman who knows how to teach. With your teaching skill, you personally can do much to help explain timestudy after you understand the reasons why. Your teaching work is made easier when there are a number of people to be studied. Explanations can be given to each in turn. You can let several days pass before you get around to adding further details. This is the best way to avoid giving your people mental indigestion.

The Right Way

Experienced men can vouch for the fact that it takes less time to explain to all those involved than it does to answer the repeated question, "Why didn't you time me?" Skilled timestudy men know that the success of work measurement is not determined by a few people. All those who work on standards should make satisfactory performances. They can do so only when they have been taught how the standards are set and have confidence in them. Therefore, it is better to explain to everyone concerned the essential parts of timestudy.

These explanations must be repeated, repeated, and repeated. They must be repeated until thoroughly understood because they have such a marked bearing upon the performances attained.

Asking Questions

Much of this educational work can be accomplished by time-study men and foremen who know how to ask questions. Asking questions is one of the practices of good teachers. That is the way they have of finding out the parts of the subject that are not understood. As applied to timestudy, the answers to questions bring out the points that are of most interest to the individual or supervisor.

In addition, misunderstandings will be revealed. Further explanations can be given to correct them. In this way, of course, the timestudy man himself will learn a lot about the people with whom he is working. He will acquire considerable knowledge about the operations in the shop. Through it all, he must be most careful to avoid giving the impression of "knowing it all."

All these are useful hints to the supervisor who wants to get ahead. You want to make certain that you don't "let George do it" and get all the experiences and skills. You want to get as much as you can for yourself. You will need a great deal more skill in "getting results through others" as you move up the ladder of promotion.

CHAPTER FOUR

Looking at the Job Details

"Why don't I get as much for this job as you gave me for the one I did yesterday? They're both the same." Note the Figure 4-1. What are you going to say when Joe Smith asks you that question? Are the jobs the same? You have to know the right answer. You have to show him that both standards are fair.

There are reasons for the difference. Chances are that it is in several small amounts. All may add together in the same direction (plus or minus). Regardless, some details in the two jobs are not the same. So the first thing to do is to compare the details. These details in timestudy are called *elements*.

Overall Time Is NG

You should not look at the two jobs as Joe does. You cannot tell where the differences are. To look at totals is an improper

Fig. 4-1. "Why don't I get as much for this job as the one I did yesterday?"

comparing of overall times. You may call these floor-to-floor times. But an overall time is not a timestudy. Such timings are worthless for at least two reasons. First, the actual time means very little without considering how diligently the person worked. Second, an overall time shows none of the details of work done or delays that occurred.

Even a "check study" must be taken in detail. Such studies are made when there is some question about a standard. The check study is almost certain to be different from the standard for several reasons.

1. Extra work may have been added.
2. Delays may be causing interference.

3. Wrong methods may be taking longer.
4. Conditions may have been changed.
5. Required effort may be lacking.

"Rate Setting"

You must be careful. You should not look at your jobs as some "rate setters" do. Sometimes, they will try to answer a question with an overall check as in Figure 4-2. Often, they carelessly

Fig. 4-2. No one can tell anything about the fairness of a standard time from an overall timing.

DRILL-PRESS OPERATION
List of Timestudy Elements—Operation 3

Correct	Combined	Condensed
Pick Up Piece		
Place In Jig	Piece In Jig	
Tighten 2 Nuts	Tighten Jig	Load In Jig
Locate Under Spl	Locate	
Lower Spindle		
Drill 1 Hole	Drill 1 Hole	Drill 1 Hole
Raise Spindle		
Move Out Jig		
Loosen 2 Nuts	Out Of Jig	
Remove Piece		
Piece Aside	Piece Aside	Unload and Aside

Fig. 4-3. There may be major differences in the lists of elements recorded on "timestudies."

combine details. You may see some combined or condensed breakdowns on so-called "timestudies." For instance, look at the comparison of three degrees of breakdowns in Figure 4-3 to see major differences.

Studies with grouped elements are worthless. They may pass for element studies because "rates" are set from them. This is because each "rate" is set by its lonesome. The "rate setter" may say to himself, "Why bother with all those details when I'll be adding the times later to get a total?" He fails to realize that a restudy will be required when some details are changed. And there will be changes. Without change, there can be no progress.

Know the Details

Whether there are changes or simple differences, you must be able to account for them. Otherwise, you cannot explain to Joe why the standards are not the same for the two jobs. Bob and Harry will have questions too. And what about Jerry, the new man you started to work the other day?

You can instruct your men properly only when you have the right details. Guessing is out when you are dealing with work measurement. You must know correctly the elements of your jobs. You need such details in order to

1. Instruct your people correctly in the methods they are to use.
2. Make certain that only the necessary elements of work are done.
3. Recognize changes in conditions that may require extra time allowances.
4. See that work eliminated from an operation is deducted from the standard.

Complete element breakdowns save time in the long run. More important, they provide the means for comparing the parts of all similar operations.

Importance of Separation

The correct separation of elements is necessary for building standard data. In this use, each element must stand by itself. Hence, a specific element must be separated from all others in an operation. If this is not done correctly, the time standards set from such elements would be in error, either high or low. Also, such elements on one study would not be comparable to similar elements on other studies. They would include different amounts of work and time.

Variations of this type often cause errors in standards when changes are made. This is because method changes usually eliminate certain elements. If those removed are credited with more or less time than they should be, then the remainder is wrong.

To repeat for emphasis, *each element must stand by itself.* Only if the timestudy separation is done correctly will

1. Elements of work in different studies be comparable to each other.
2. Element standards be fair for setting present and future operation standards.
3. Elements of setup be identified and separated from productive standards.
4. Extra work and delay times be separated from productive operations.
5. Elements that are not necessary be excluded from correct standards.

Separate Elements

For the reasons just stated, the timestudy man or the foreman-in-training must take detailed timestudies. This he must do because every shop operation is a combination of elementary motions. Some are necessary. Others are wasted time and effort. None can be recorded in combination. And study is of prime importance because one object is to reduce waste of all kinds. Then too, there is the basic question asked at the opening of this chapter. To answer it correctly requires a proper comparison of details. Notice Figure 4-4. Some may be alike. Others will be different. These comparisons can be made only in the details taken on good timestudies. Such timestudies

1. Record exactly all the elements of work done.
2. Assist in further analysis of like operations.
3. Separate waste and delay from necessary work.
4. Provide for a comparison of elements of similar operations.

Fig. 4-4. You will have a "helluva" time explaining job differences without correct element breakdowns.

Element Definition

Thus far, much emphasis has been placed on the need for correct element breakdown. At this point, it might be proper to define the term "element."

> *An element is a basic part of an operation observed in timestudy and consists of several motions regularly done in the same sequence to accomplish a definite result.*

Elements are the same for all like operations performed under identical conditions. For example, they are the parts of the jobs that make a "lathe hand." They are the details of work that are found everywhere in similar trades. They are the basic parts of a trade skill.

Elements are of two distinct types. These are called "constants" and "variables." These terms are almost self-explanatory. Just the same, definitions will be given so that the meanings of the words will be clear.

Constant Element

A constant is an element related to a specified set of conditions and has a standard time that is always the same.

On a drill press of a certain size and make, Raise Spindle and Lock Feed are examples. Constant times present little or no difficulty in their determination. They are fixed by certain working conditions. However, they sometimes confuse a timestudy man because he finds it so convenient to combine two or more constants in one watch reading. Perhaps these can be separated later. But it is better practice to take the study correctly.

Just for emphasis, let me cite what a constant is not. Two or more elements that have the same times on different studies are not likely to be constants. They may be variable elements that have the same dimension factors.

Variable Element

In contrast with constants, variable elements are the primary concern of the timestudy man. Note carefully the definition.

A variable is an element whose time standard should change to allow for differences in the dimensions of the product or process.

Drill press variables might be Pick Up Piece, Hole to Hole, and Turn over Jig. Variables are the real problems in timestudy. They control the changes in standards from one size to another. Take note. Variables cause most of the differences between standards for similar parts.

Again, let's point out the negative. An element is not a

variable just because it has different times on the same or on
several studies. Maybe the conditions were different. Perhaps
the person being studied changed his pace. Maybe the watch
was not read at the same points in the cycles. Keep in mind
that element times recorded on the study are results. They are
effects.

Breakdown Example

The two kinds of elements may be illustrated by comparing
the listings of purchases at the supermarket as shown in Figure
4-5. Observe that the total bills are $8.03 in both cases. But
that does not mean that the family supplies are the same. As
a matter of fact, they are quite different. The lists are not alike
for two reasons.

1. Some items differ because of price.
2. Certain costs vary because of amounts.

Saturday Groceries	Purchases		"Elements" Typify	
	Jones	Smith	Constant	Variable
Eggs	$ .57	$ .57	Eggs	
Milk	.31	.31	Milk	
Coffee	.85	.97		Coffee
Cheese	.40	.55		Cheese
Soup	.24	.24	Soup	
Tomato	.39	.55		Tomato
Bread	.41	.41	Bread	
Oranges	.79	.79	Oranges	
Meat	1.85	1.10		Meat
Candy	.30	.50		Candy
Cake	1.50	1.50	Cake	
Smokes	.42	.54		Smokes
	$8.03	$8.03		

Fig. 4-5. Two lists of groceries may contain elements that are alike (constants)
and others that are different (variables).

The items that are the same are noted in the column headed Constant. The supplies that differ are recorded in the Variable column. This simple breakdown of the differences between two lists of groceries may help to explain element analysis.

Detailing an Operation

If one of these lists were your grocery bill, you might study it to see where you could reduce it. If you paid both, you would compare them, looking for those purchases that were extravagant. Both methods are like those used in timestudy. The study of a shop operation begins with an itemized listing of its elements. These may be short enough to average 20 per minute. The breakdown really is in detail. For instance, a study of a simple drill press operation might show the elements noted in Figure 4-6.

Drill Press Elements Operation 3	Class of Element (when comparing one job with another)	
	Constant	Variable
Pick Up Piece.............	....	Weight-distance
Place in Jig...............	....	Size-design
Tighten 2 Nuts.............	....	Kind-size
Locate under Spl...........	....	Weight-setup
Lower Spindle.............	Machine type	
Drill 1 Hole...............	....	Size, length, etc.
Raise Spindle.............	Machine type	
Move Out Jig.............	.. ..	Weight-distance
Loosen 2 Nuts.............	....	Kind-size
Remove Piece.............	....	Size-design
Piece Aside...............	....	Weight-distance

Fig. 4-6. Element listing for Operation 3 on a drill press.

Beginning a Study

Such a listing is the start of a timestudy. It might be made while watching the production of several pieces. It might take that long to record carefully all elements. Some skilled timestudy men can make the breakdown while timing. This becomes necessary when studying work like setup and maintenance operations. The timestudy man must write the elements and read his watch as the job moves along because

1. There is only one cycle in the usual nonrepetitive job.
2. There can be no meaningful listing of elements in advance.

Reading Point

The element breakdown tends to fix the lengths of the watch readings. They should correspond. For the element times to be correct, the timestudy man must read his watch at the proper points in the operation. These are called *reading points.* Naturally, the watch reading points should correspond with the element descriptions. *The reading points are the beginnings of the elements.* Notice that element ending is not mentioned. The reason is that the beginning of an element is the ending of the preceding one.

The reading points are specified conversely by work content descriptions like those shown in Figure 4-7. Some reading points are easily noticed, as clicks or other operation noises. Some are much less definite. To illustrate, the reading point must be defined in order to separate the two drill press elements Remove from Jig and Piece Aside. These two elements are performed almost as one continuous motion. Yet, two such variable elements must be recorded separately because they vary for different reasons. The time to unload the jig is determined by the design of the jig and the shape and size of the part. The handling of the piece depends upon its weight and a varying

ELEMENT DESCRIPTION

Pick Up Piece

Begins When operator starts to reach for piece of work.

Includes Pick up and transporting of piece.

Ends When piece is in position to be placed in jig or fixture.

Load in Jig

Begins When operator starts to insert piece in jig or fixture.

Includes Placing and locating of piece in jig or fixture.

Ends When work is placed correctly in jig or fixture.

Remove Piece

Begins When man starts reaching for piece in jig or other holding or locating device.

Includes All work necessary to loosen piece from studs, pins, or other locating devices.

Ends When piece can be easily removed from jig or holding device.

Piece Aside

Begins When man starts taking piece out or away from jig or fixture.

Includes Lift to take out, transport, and laying aside of piece.

Ends After work is placed on table, box, or can, and hand is free to do other work.

Fig. 4-7. Precise descriptions of the work contents of elements are very necessary to explain the shorthand notes on the timestudies.

distance of piece aside. To provide for the separation of such elements, specifications like those shown in Figure 4-7 are written.

Description Shorthand

Now let me point out a difference you should understand. First, compare the element descriptions written in Figure 4-7 with the drill press elements for Operation 3 recorded in Figure 4-6. For example, observe the two-word notation Piece Aside in both illustrations. Then make a mental note. The two- or three-word element description written on a timestudy is only "shorthand" writing. Sometimes, the timestudy moves so fast that only element initials can be recorded. You can see that these brief notes do not *describe* the elements.

Future References

Obviously, you need more complete element specifications for future references. Sometime or other, you must have exact descriptions of the work that was included in the times because

1. They are useful when standards are to be changed for revision in the methods.
2. They are very helpful for instructing when you have new men to train.
3. They are necessary when you are trying to observe differences between people.
4. They are important to you in "seeing" how an operation is actually done.

What to Look for

Remember that not everybody "sees" what he is looking at. But when you stand behind a watch, the detailed elements magnify the operation. Any job appears to you much the same as if you were looking at it through a magnifying glass. Some details will surprise you. Some don't belong. Some need to be improved. And many questions immediately flash into mind. The questions the timestudy man might think of could be like those shown in Figure 4-8.

WHY do the parts have to be that far away?

START....

WHY did they use two nuts when one is enough?

WHY need the jig be so hard to load?

Pick up piece
Place in jig
Tighten 2 nuts
Locate under sol.
Lower spindle
Drill one hole
Raise spindle
Move out jig
Loosen 2 nuts
Remove piece
Piece aside

WHY is the head set so far from the table?

WHY not set up some locating stops?

WHY does the bushing come up?

WHY is the drill running at that speed?

WHY turn the nuts so many extra threads?

WHY is the table three feet wide?

WHY do the chips inter-fere so much?

WHY are the parts put aside so carefully?

·STOP----------

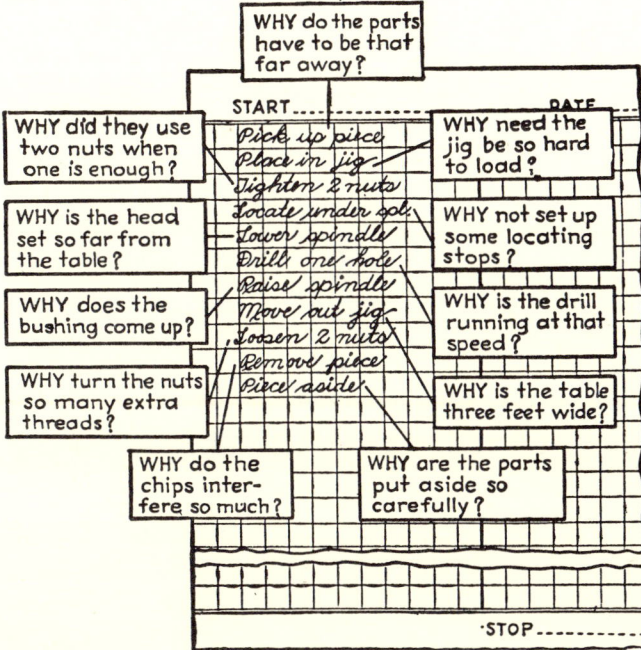

Fig. 4-8. The skilled timestudy man has many questions to ask about operations he is observing.

The answers to such questions often lead to better ways of doing work. They bring out ideas that can also be applied to other jobs. However, you can't do this sort of job analysis without becoming progressive. You can't suggest better methods and still say, "We always did it that way." Hence, when you begin to see the details of your operations as the timestudy man views them, you are on your way up. Recognize that training in element analysis will greatly improve your ability to observe correctly

1. That a considerable part of the time is spent in Get Ready and Put Away.

2. That each working minute is made up of a great many small elements of time.

3. That perhaps only one-third of the time is used in doing the productive part of the job.

4. That the unplanned operation layout uses up too much energy in reaching and bending over.

5. That you can improve many of the elements in many jobs without help from anybody.

6. That when the man is working, the machine is usually idle, or the reverse.

7. That many an operation started to fix some bad lot of material is still going on.

8. That most jigs were designed to last 100 years rather than to give easy operation.

CHAPTER FIVE

How Long Does It Take?

"It took me over an hour to make 12 pieces. I had bad luck with one of 'em," Bill told me. But his measure was an overall clock time. Such a timing tells us no more about the job than a timekeeper's record of a sporting event.

Common Misconception

Can you find the game timekeeper's account on the sports page? Sometimes, if it is extra long. But do you pay any attention to the record he makes as in Figure 5-1? Certainly not. You're interested in who scored, not how long the game lasted. You care only to know what happened during the time. The same is true in timestudy.

An overall "stop watch" timing tells us nothing of value. Bill is off on the wrong foot in talking about overall clock time. Here are some of the possible reasons:

Fig. 5-1. You have little interest in the timekeeper's record of a football game.

Maybe the material wasn't good.
Maybe the tools were not right.
Maybe the method used was wrong.
Maybe the time included delays.
Maybe Bill was out late last night.

Detail Timing

You must know what causes excess time. And the easiest way
to find out is to look at all the details. For instance, note the
lost time in Figure 5-2. The small details in timestudy are those
we named *elements* in the previous chapter. Each one of them
affects the total time. Each one should be studied. How
long does each one take? Observing the time for each element is called *watch reading*. That is our next step in timestudy.

Fig. 5-2. One falsity of actual time is seen in this example of a machine "cutting wind."

Types of Watches

To get element watch readings, we use what everybody calls a "stopwatch." The usual kinds are divided into seconds or decimals. The "second" watch is rarely used in timestudy. Most timestudy men prefer decimal watches. These are of two kinds. One type is arranged to show decimal hours. The other, perhaps the most widely used watch, is the kind that reads in decimal parts of a minute.

Purpose of Watch Readings

The reason for recording the small time divisions from the "stopwatch" is to break down the "overall" time. We want to find out how long each element takes. Each element time is a decimal part of the total if a decimal watch is used. The total may be longer or shorter than it should be. Therefore, the time taken for each element is apt to be more or less than it ought to be. For example, if the total is 80 percent of a normal time, then perhaps each of the elements will be 80 percent of a normal time. Often in good timestudy, this is true.

Rarely will the actual times be those required by the normal qualified operator. They can be normal only when a normal qualified operator works at a normal pace. The most important point to remember about watch reading is that the time recorded on the study is simply the *actual time taken.*

Decimal Minute Watch

Most timestudy watches have two hands. The small hand indicates minutes on a dial graduated to show 30 for one revolution. The large sweep hand is the one used for reading element

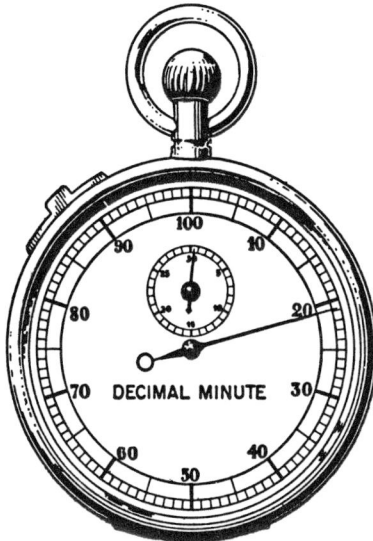

Fig. 5-3. Each one of the divisions of the outside circle of markings on a decimal minute watch is .01 minute.

times. It points to the decimal parts of a minute on a large dial that contains 100 divisions. You can see these in Figure 5-3.

Incidentally, the decimal hour watch looks exactly like this. However, the large hand makes 1.67 revolutions per minute. This feature permits the taking of slightly more accurate readings. But this advantage is quickly lost in the added burden of carrying two extra decimal places throughout all calculations. Besides, the four decimal places confuse many employees.

The two-decimal-place standards set in minutes are more understandable. They look like the cents figures on the paycheck, grocery bill, and gas station meter.

Two Kinds of Watch Readings

In taking studies, there are two commonly used methods of reading the watch. One is called "continuous" watch reading. The other is named "snapback." Both methods have their uses. Both have advantages as well as disadvantages. A comparison of these two types of watch readings can be made by studying Figure 5-4 made up from turret lathe studies.

Continuous Watch Reading

Continuous watch readings are like the ones you make every day when you look at the clock. If you read your watch frequently while you were waiting for your wife, you might remember times like

10:11	10:18	10:32	10:46	10:53
10:15	10:25	10:41	10:50	10:58

Such time readings are similar to those you find on any airplane or railroad timetable. They give the arrival time at each stop as part of a schedule in Figure 5-5.

WATCH READING

SNAPBACK   CONTINUOUS

.06   Pick up Piece   .06

.05   Place in Collet   .11

.04   Tighten Collet   .15

.04   Guard Down   .19

.03   Start Machine   .22

.10   Turret Up.   .32

.32   Total   .32

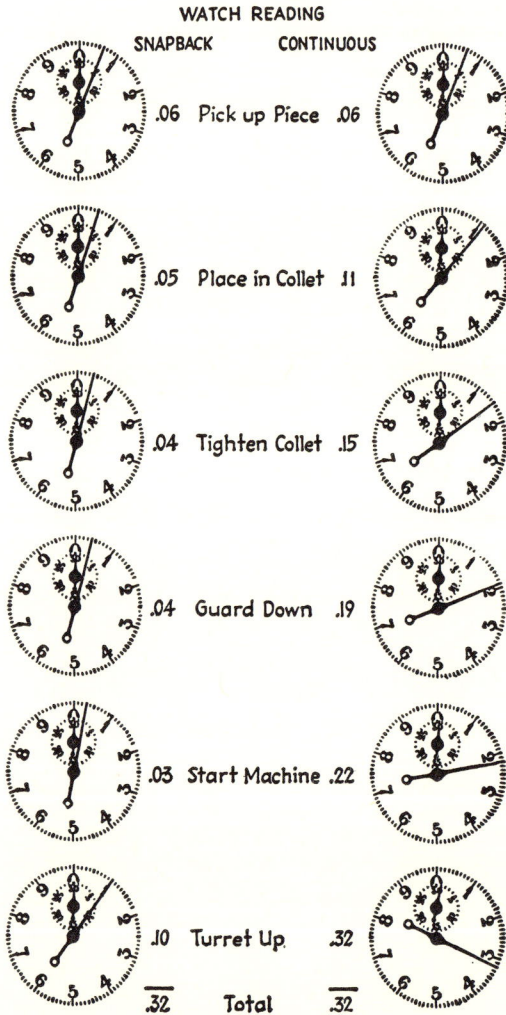

Fig. 5-4. Comparison of snapback and continuous watch readings.

25	Miles	Station	26
2:19	3	Tower Grove	11:14
3:19	45	De Sota	9:50
4:08	79	Bismarck	9:02
4:26	92	Ironton	8:38
5:17	130	Piedmont	7:42
6:15	169	Poplar Bluff	6:50

Fig. 5-5. Part of a railroad timetable that shows "continuous" watch readings.

These continuous watch readings are said to have greater accuracy. These claims have merit. However, the small gain in accuracy is not worth all the extra clerical cost. Element times can be obtained only by subtracting one watch reading from another. Not only is this very costly; it involves some errors. In attempting to avoid part of this wasted effort, some "rate setters" try to subtract times during their studies. Such practice is faulty. The observer cannot concentrate on his main job of timestudy and also do clerical work.

Uses of Continuous Method

Nevertheless, the continuous method may be used for two types of timestudy. First, it may be best when elements are extremely short. Such elements are those having times like .01 and .02 minutes. Second, the continuous method is recommended when timing several people working together. The continuous method is more advantageous because the clerical work can be done in the office. Timestudies can be made of groups by the snapback method. This requires much more writing of elements during the study.

The major disadvantage of the continuous watch reading is that the observer has no knowledge of actual times. He is not

| | SNAPBACK | | | | | CONTINUOUS | | | | |
START _10:20_	RATE _75_					RATE _75_				
Pick up piece	02	03	03	04	03	02	57	14	73	34
Place in jig	04	05	05	06	05	06	62	19	79	39
Tighten 2 screws	05	06	06	07	05	11	68	25	76	44
Locate under spl.	03	02	02	03	03	14	70	27	79	47
Lower spindle	03	02	03	02	02	17	72	30	91	49
Drill one hole HF	26	26	25	27	26	43	98	55	218	75
Raise spindle	02	01	02	01	02	45	99	57	19	77
Loosen 2 screws	04	05	05	06	05	49	104	62	25	82
Remove piece	03	04	04	04	04	52	08	66	29	86
Piece aside	02	03	03	02	03	54	11	69	31	289

STOP _10:23_   STOP _10:23_

Fig. 5-6. Notice the differences in elapsed times under the snapback that are not revealed during the study by the continuous watch readings.

alerted to either changes in work content or to alterations in work pace. Compare the two types of watch readings shown in Figure 5-6.

Snapback Watch Reading

The bulk of timestudy watch reading should be made by the snapback method. The subtracting is done automatically by returning the large hand to zero at the end of each element. The watch is read at the end of the element and the stem is pressed down. This action returns the hand to zero, which immediately becomes the start of the next element. Thus, the snapback watch readings are actual elapsed times. These actuals are of major concern to the observer because he can see what is taking place. He notices whether the times are varying and to what extent. This enables him to do a much better job of *rating the performance* shown by the operator. Rating is the subject of our next chapter.

Short Element Times

Correctly taken watch readings are short. Otherwise, the study is not properly broken down into detailed elements. Many element times are about .05 minute. Some are longer. Those that are longer than .05 should be analyzed. They may contain two or more elements. Combined elements should be separated even if the study has been in progress for some time. This is readily done by inserting the newly separated element in proper sequence. Its corresponding times are then recorded between lines.

Reading the Watch

Reading the watch is an instantaneous mental noting of the position of the large hand at the end of each element. Immediately thereafter, the large hand is snapped back to zero to begin timing the next element. The speed of snapback is critical. Speed reduces the percent error in watch reading to almost nothing.

1. The snapback movement must be done subconsciously, nearly automatically.
2. The sweep hand must be returned to zero with practically no loss in time.
3. Zero is the start of the next element that follows in the timestudy.

Time Errors

Watch reading is like any other operation. It requires considerable skill to do it correctly. Errors may occur for several reasons.

1. The timestudy man may be slow in snapping back the watch.
2. The observer may read the watch incorrectly or at a wrong time in the cycle.
3. The large hand may be allowed to continue after the reading has been made.
4. The watch may be read correctly, but a different figure is recorded.
5. The miscellaneous element times may be omitted, thereby making the study incomplete.

Incorrect Watch Reading

When the watch is not read correctly, the times will vary for identical elements. One observer might get unlike readings on several studies of the same operation. Several timestudy men can get different times for the same element. A simple illustration may emphasize the point. In Figure 5-7, five elements are

Element	Study 1	Study 2	Study 3
A	.05	.07	.06
B	.09	.07	.10
C	.12	.13	.11
D	.06	.04	.03
E	.08	.09	.10
Total	.40	.40	.40

Fig. 5-7. Three short studies show the same total times, but observe the differences among the element times.

recorded for each of three studies taken of one operator. The totals are identical, but the individual element times differ.

The example is intended to show only errors in watch readings. Notice in this chart that

1. Element A in Study 2 includes 40 percent more time than Element A in Study 1.
2. Element E in Study 3 contains 25 percent more time than Element E in Study 1.

What's the Difference

The next question might be, "What difference does it make since the totals are the same?" The answer is, "Considerable." Suppose, for instance, that Element A is one that is done in every job on several departments. Assume the remaining four elements do not occur very often. According to the element times, the job allowance might be more or less than fair.

Suppose another condition that frequently happens. Imagine a change in method, equipment, or design that eliminates Elements B and D. To see what will result, take a look at Figure 5-8. The new totals are .25, .29, and .27. There is a difference between Study 1 and Study 2 of 16 percent. Which time should we use? Such differences in times destroy the true comparisons of elements.

Element	Study 1	Study 2	Study 3
A	.05	.07	.06
C	.12	.13	.11
E	.08	.09	.10
Total	.25	.29	.27

Fig. 5-8. Notice the differences in totals when Elements B and D (shown in Figure 5-7) are omitted.

Full Concentration

From the discussion thus far, it should be apparent that the watch must be read at the right points in the cycle. Otherwise, the element times will be wrong. Consider the fact also that if one element is read "long" and the next one is read correctly, both times are in error.

To take good timestudies requires a high degree of concentration. Besides, considerable practice is necessary in order to achieve practical accuracy in snapback watch reading. The best results are attained by using the index finger for depressing the watch stem. It is the most skilled finger of the hand.

In addition, some checks of correctness are necessary. One test and practice device is the "trainer" I invented that is sold by Meylan Stopwatch. It consists of discs having correctly calibrated pie-shaped segments in colors. These are turned at one revolution per minute by an electric clock motor. Thus, the "element" times are exact.

Complete Study

The watch should not be stopped at all during the study, as the term "stopwatch" might indicate. It must be allowed to run throughout the entire period of observation. And everything that takes place during the study must be recorded. When these specifications are followed, then the total elapsed time can be accounted for. The total is the difference between the start and stop times of the study.

Start and Stop Times

The time when the study is started should be recorded at the beginning of the study. The "stop" time ought to be noted at the end. Both start and stop times should be recorded on all studies.

The difference between these times is the total elapsed time taken. It should equal the sum of all readings on the study. This is another and a different test of watch reading accuracy.

When these two total times are not alike, the recorded element times are not correct or are not complete or both. The sum of the recorded times may be lower. That is because of errors and omissions. To reduce such errors, the completeness of each study should be checked until the comparison of the two total times shows practically no mistakes.

The start and stop times serve other purposes. They show the time of day when the timestudy was taken. Also, they provide the means for obtaining quick answers to the length of time of observation.

Group Timestudy

Before going on, I want to touch upon group timestudy mentioned earlier in this chapter. First, take a look at Figure 5-9.

Fig. 5-9. If each man here represents an element on a timestudy, think how important it is to correctly time each one.

There you will see ten men assigned to a project. Now imagine that each man represents one element of an operation. Then ask yourself these questions.

1. Would an actual time taken give me any facts about the job?
2. Would a study of one man tell me what the group was doing?
3. Would a change in the number of men affect the amount of work done?

To learn how much work there is in the job, you must correctly time what each man does. This corresponds with proper element timing. Then you must judge the pace that each man works during the study. Again, this is called *rating performance*.

From this example, two facts about group timestudy should be apparent.

1. The amount of work is unbalanced among the men, hence idle time is present.
2. The work done shifts among the men, therefore all must be studied at the same time.

Recording the Times

Getting back to element study, usually these are listed one after another in sequence like names on the payroll. Then, the study is completed by recording the watch readings beside the corresponding elements. Often the elements are few in number. Five to twenty make up the repetitive types of operations. In such short studies, perhaps 20 watch readings would be noted for each element.

In making his study, the observer holds his board and watch

in a position that permits him to see both the watch and the operation. He critically observes the work being done and the method being used. At the same time, the observer's eyes are keeping pace with the watch hand as it moves around. In this way, each watch reading he writes on the study is really the last one of several mentally noted.

While studying non-repetitive work, the timestudy man must be especially alert. Jobs like setup, for example, consist of long series of elements with only *one watch reading each.* Still others, like certain assembly operations, may contain a mixture. Some elements might have one reading each while others have several. All such conditions must be considered in order that the study be taken to reduce the clerical work in the steps to follow.

Simple Timestudy Sheet

To record the timestudy, you need some kind of paper. Most of us think immediately of a form. Don't rush. One of the best engineers I ever knew used only plain sheets of 5½ by 8½ inch scratch pad.

If a sheet is to be designed, the varied kinds of timestudies should be taken into account. A flexible and satisfactory sheet can be made that looks like ordinary squared paper. Quarter-inch squares allow ample space for watch readings. The lines are far enough apart for element descriptions. Such rulings do not limit the form of the study. Elements may be written down the left side of the page or across the top. Watch readings can be recorded in any spaces available. Four ways to use the sheet are shown on one page illustrated as Figure 5-10. The sheet can be made in any practical size. What is recommended is the 5½ by 8½ inch sheet, half of a standard letter-sized page.

START__	REPEATING CYCLES MANY ELEMENTS			RATE__	SHORT REPEATING OPERATIONS FEW ELEMENTS										
Pick up piece	02	03													
Place in jig	04	05													
Tighten 2 screws	05	06													
Locate under spl.	03	02													
Lower spindle	03	02													
Drill one hole HF	26	26													
Raise spindle	02	01													
Loosen 2 screws	04	05													
Remove piece	03	04	02	04	05	03	03	26	02	04	03	02			
Piece aside	02	03	03	05	06	02	02	26	01	05	04	03			

(Vertical column headings in SHORT REPEATING OPERATIONS section: Pick up piece, Place in jig, Tighten 2 screws, Locate under spindle, Lower spindle, Drill one hole, Raise spindle, Loosen 2 screws, Remove piece, Piece aside)

SET-UP AND NON-REPETITIVE TIMESTUDY			ASSEMBLY AND OPERATIONS WITH REPEATING ELEMENTS				
Remove tool	12		Pick up piece	06			
Clean machine	34		Place in fixture	05			
Remove chuck	42		Tighten fixture	05			
Place in rack	15		Get name plate	03			
Get material	73		Place	04			
Read drawing	41		Get drill	08			
Set stop	22		Drill hole	05	06	05	05
Select stock	14		Drill aside	06			
Set tool	11		Get ham., pins	05			
Bring up tailstock	13		Drive esc. pin	03	02	03	03
Set pc. in center	10		Hammer aside	03			
Start machine	04		Loosen fixture	05			
Run in tool	05		Piece aside	04			
Lock feed	03						
Trial cut	28						

STOP_____

Fig. 5-10. A simply designed timestudy sheet that can be used for recording several types of observations.

Advantages of Element Times

Just to emphasize, make sure that you do not think watch reading is the whole of timestudy. There are many more vital phases you should keep in mind.

1. Knowledge of elements of work vastly increases your regard for the value of time.
2. Comparisons of one operation with others can be made because the studies are in elements.
3. Elements timed in many jobs are found to be the same regardless of the operation done.
4. Delays that interfere with production are much more noticeable on correctly made timestudies.
5. Extra work done because of faulty materials is seen as interferences with productive output.
6. Time lost due to excess walking becomes much more evident when closely studied.
7. Time spent to Get Ready and Put Away stands out like a "sore thumb."
8. Idle time resulting from unbalanced operations in a group is readily seen.

CHAPTER SIX

How Long Should It Take?

"How long does it take you to mow your lawn?" "That depends," you would say if I asked you that question. Your answer would be proper. The time would depend upon whether you used a hand or a power mower. The time would be longer if your lawn mower were not in good shape. The time would change if you were not in "good shape." It would depend upon how anxious you were to get the job done, as suggested by Figure 6-1, the tools you used, and the method you followed. The same is true in the performing of a shop operation.

Timestudy Actuals

Surely we can say that the actual time you take to cut your grass is likely to differ from one weekend to the next. If you kept track of your times for several weeks in a row, you would have a time card of actuals.

Fig. 6-1. The "how long" it takes you to mow your lawn depends upon the effort you make.

Such entries on your time card are just like the actual times written on a timestudy. The only difference is in the amount of detail. But the time that was taken may be far from the *right time*. For work measurement purposes, the timestudy man must set the time that *should* be taken. He must consider two kinds of differences. First are the differences in methods that may result from variations in working conditions, tooling, and skill of the operator. Second are the differences in performances that are caused by changes in pace of working.

Method and Pace

Correctly taken timestudies permit the observer to separate method from pace. Method causes the number and kind of elements in an operation. Pace causes the rate of performing those elements whatever they may be. Naturally, both method and pace have their influence on the time taken and the time required. Both affect output per hour. For instance, you know that methods improvement can increase output. That's why you are always trying to find better ways.

However, at any given stage of progress, the timestudy man can *record only what he sees.* As a result, his studies will contain mixtures of methods and rates of performing them. Thus, he must

1. Record the *elements of work done,* and
2. *Rate the pace* of work performance

Average Time

Considering these factors, the timestudy man should not use average times. These are decidedly wrong. There is no direct connection between "time taken" and a fair standard. For example, the average of actual times taken at 40 percent of normal pace would equal a 40 percent of normal time. Likewise, an average of a 200 percent actual times would allow only half of the normal time required by a normal operator. A look at Figure 6-2 should clearly indicate to you the error of using averages.

The examples are of a simple drill press operation. Study A is of a subnormal operator (rating 35/60 or 58 percent). Study B is of an individual working at the pace usually attained under incentive (rating 75/60 or 125 percent).

Compare the averages of the five actual times shown at the right sides of the studies. Incidentally, the drilling was done by

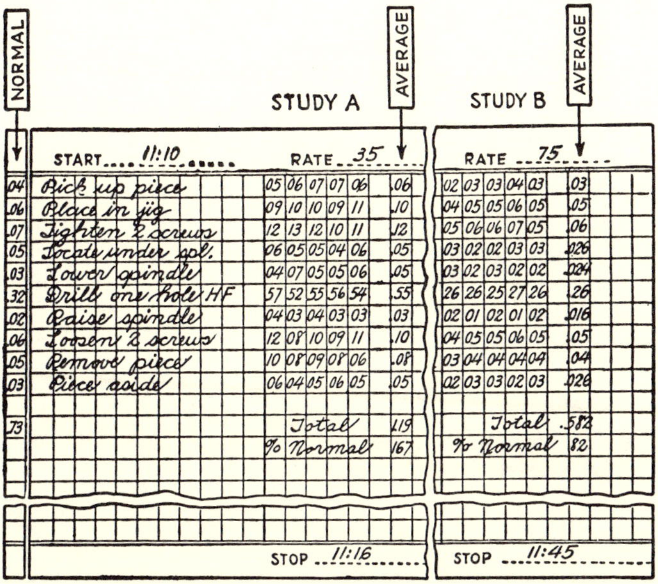

Fig. 6-2. Two studies of the same operation showing average times that result from differences in work pace.

hand feed. It is assumed that the machining is affected by the effort to the same extent as the handling times.

The figures clearly show that the *average times are wrong* as a basis for setting standards. Not only are these two sets of average times different from each other. Also, both of them differ from the normal times shown at the extreme left under the heading Normal. From this example, it should be obvious that average times do not produce fair element normal times. (Relax has been left out of these examples to avoid confusion.)

Differences in Timestudies

From the preceding discussion, it should be evident that two major variables may be included in any study. Among studies, both method and pace may vary as shown by the examples

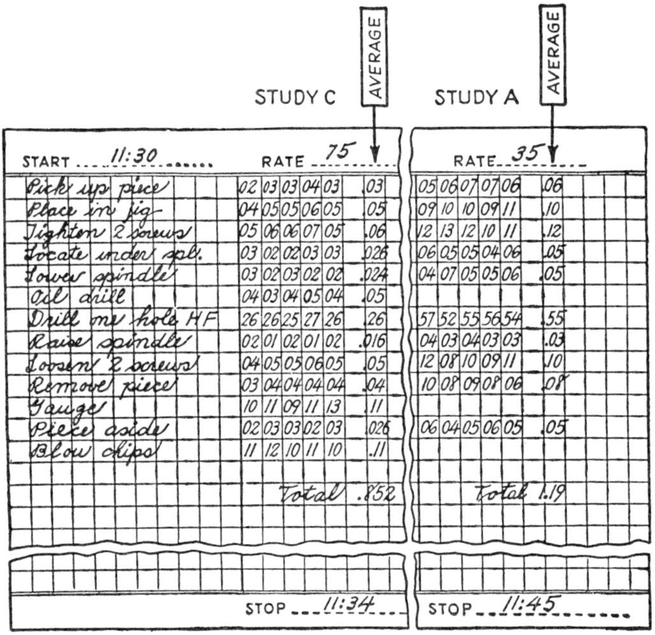

Fig. 6-3. Two studies with average times that illustrate differences in method.

Study C and Study A in Figure 6-3. Study C includes three elements of work that were not found in Study A. And yet, the total average time of Study C is much less. The operator worked more rapidly. (The pace rating in Study C is higher.) From these examples, it should be clear also that you should not juggle pace ratings to adjust for method differences.

Standard Data Method

To avoid the variety of possible inconsistencies, good time-study practice is to build *standard data*. This is done before any job standards are set. The method involves three steps.

1. Rating paces of performances on all studies in terms of a normal pace.
2. Taking many studies to sample the ranges of work in the trade.
3. Selecting the methods that will be standard for the operations.

Now recall, the timestudy man can study only what he sees. Thus, he rates the pace of performing those elements (method) that are done. This step results in element times at normal pace. These can be compared. Then later, the required element standards (method) for the normal method can be added together to set job standards.

Reasons for Rating

As just outlined, rating takes place before methods are considered in the standard data process. So let's discuss rating first. The reasons for rating are many. The chief one is to determine fair element times. Fair element times must be established from a wide range of actual times. Some operators perform as low as 40 percent of normal. A few work as effectively as 200 percent of the same normal.

These same people will show considerable variation in times within any one study. There may be as much as 60 percent difference between the least and the greatest time observed for each element. Also, the times for the elements may be as much as 60 percent greater at the beginning or ending of the day than on either side of lunchtime. Besides, everyone knows the effects of "blue Monday."

Regardless, elements that are alike should have corresponding time standards. Hence, to get fair standards, you must adjust the actual times for differences in pace. The times for the elements recorded may vary with:

1. The time of day when the study was taken.
2. The day of the week the observing was done.
3. The pace the operator worked at during study.

Considering all these variations, it should be apparent that pace rating must be used. Trained judgment must be applied. There is no other practical way known for relating the actions of human beings to standards of normal time.

What Is Rating

Rating is somewhat like measuring weight with a scale. Different people stepping on a scale would be expected to weigh differently. The weight of any one person would change from time to time. In a similar way, the times recorded for the elements of a timestudy will vary with the same operator and with different ones.

From these varying times, the timestudy man must select times that represent normal. This he does by judging the relation between the performances he sees and the normal, and then noting the rating factor on his studies. So, rating is the gauging of the operator's pace during the timestudy in terms of a normal pace.

Attitude toward Timestudy

Of course, the pace of the individual will be affected by his attitude toward timestudy and the timestudy man. If mutual confidence exists, he may work at his usual pace. He may speed up, as suggested by Figure 6-4. On the other hand, if he is agin' work measurement, he may slow down. Regardless of such changes, the timestudy man is expected to set fair element

Fig. 6-4. The actual time may be low because the individual studied worked diligently.

times. This he can do when he has been trained to rate the performances demonstrated by the producer during the study.

Normal Pace

The rating is in terms of *normal*. The normal used should conform with the amount of work expected in return for the wage paid. That statement may be a little confusing because base rates vary with conditions. Naturally, the definition of normal does not change with rising base rates. Remember, however, we do say "a fair day's work for a fair day's pay."

Perhaps a better way of expressing the relation would be in terms of time. *The normal is the amount of work that should be done in one unit of time.* This normal pace is a standard of expectancy that the timestudy man mentally compares to the performance observed. Some specify this pace as equivalent to dealing 52 cards in bridge hands in .45 minute. The comparison is made during the timestudy. The resulting rating factor is noted on the study. It is sometimes expressed in terms of percent with 100 representing normal. In many plants, it is shown in terms of 60 standard minutes as normal.

Applying the Rating

For example, the rating 35 means that the performance was judged to be 35/60 (57 percent) of a fair day's work. In applying this factor, the selected times are multiplied by 35/60. This calculation reduces the actual time taken to that considered normal operation. In contrast, the application of the factor 75/60 adds to the actual time, as seen in Figure 6-5.

Similar results are shown next to their descriptions for all elements of the studies in Figure 6-6. There you can see that practically the same standard times are determined from both studies. You recognize the necessity for attaining such consistency in element times. Keep in mind then that rating is probably the most important step in the technical part of

Study	Element	Actual		Rating	Normal
A	Pick Up Piece	.07	X	35/60 (57%)	.04 min.
B	Pick Up Piece	.03	X	75/60 (125%)	.04 min.

Fig. 6-5. Examples of the use of rating factors to convert actual times to normal times.

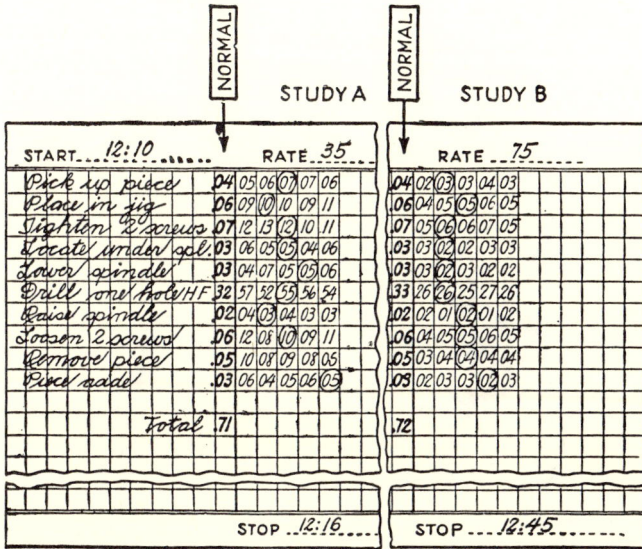

STUDY A — NORMAL — RATE 35
STUDY B — NORMAL — RATE 75

START 12:10

Element	Normal						Normal					
Pick up piece	04	05	06	07	07	06	04	02	03	03	04	03
Place in jig	06	09	10	10	09	11	06	04	05	05	06	05
Tighten 2 screws	07	12	13	12	10	11	07	05	06	06	07	05
Locate under spl.	03	06	05	05	04	06	03	03	02	02	03	03
Lower spindle	03	04	07	05	05	06	03	03	02	03	02	02
Drill one hole/HF	32	57	52	55	56	54	33	26	26	25	27	26
Raise spindle	02	04	03	04	03	03	02	02	01	02	01	02
Loosen 2 screws	06	12	08	10	09	11	06	04	05	05	06	05
Remove piece	05	10	08	09	08	05	05	03	04	04	04	04
Piece aside	03	06	04	05	06	05	05	02	03	03	02	03
Total	71						72					

STOP 12:16   STOP 12:45

Fig. 6-6. Timestudies showing normal times determined from performances of widely differing paces.

timestudy. Its importance lies in the effect that proper rating has upon the measurement of a fair day's work.

Relax Must Be Added

The normal times shown on the preceding studies do not contain any allowances for relax. Relax is a term that means the sum of personal and fatigue allowances. It was omitted from the examples in order to portray only the adjustments for rating.

But element standards should contain personal and fatigue allowances to be fair to the employees. Otherwise, an individual could not maintain his pace "day in and day out."

Fig. 6-7. Relax factors are added to normal times to allow for "day in and day out" performances.

Note Figure 6-7. Factors in it vary according to the type of work done. The allowance might be 10 percent for benchwork and increase according to working conditions to 35 percent for strenuous foundry work, for example. Higher factors are sometimes necessary. For instance, what is a fair relax factor for the man who runs the 100-yard dash?

Study	Element	Actual	Rating	Relax	Standard
A	Loosen 2 screws	.10	$\frac{35}{60}$	$+ 15\%$	$= .07$ min.
B	Loosen 2 screws	.05	$\frac{75}{60}$	$+ 15\%$	$= .07$ min.

Fig. 6-8. Examples of different actuals converted to normal times with relax added to produce like element standards.

The 10 to 35 percent range indicates percentages commonly used. Such factors are applied when working up the study at the same time as the rating factors. The arithmetic is like that shown in Figure 6-8.

Element Standard Time

By the method just described, the actual watch readings are converted to standard times. Attention is called to the fact that allowances for relax are added into each element standard. This method is preferred because

1. Standard data is built upon the basis that each of the elements stands by itself.
2. Relax is added in the same calculation with rating to save clerical work.
3. Relax is applied according to the fatiguing effects of the elements of effort.

After the conversions are made and the allowances added, the timestudy observations are complete. These standard times should be written on the timestudy beside the element descriptions. They should be noted with a colored pencil so they can be distinguished easily.

Various Methods

In the finished timestudy, the observer might note that there were some variations from usual methods. As Frank Gilbreth discovered, a bricklayer used three different ones.

1. The method he showed while instructing an apprentice.
2. The method he used when someone was watching him.
3. The method he applied when he was working alone.

Such variations are not seen in a single timestudy. But they are readily noticed when many studies are compared.

Taking a Trip

You will note the differences that can occur from a simple example. Suppose you had to go from Kansas City to Omaha. You might have a choice of several ways to travel. Perhaps you could drive, fly, or take a train. If you chose to drive, there are a number of routes shown on the map in Figure 6-9.

The method differences may be thought of as the different routes or the different vehicles.

The pace differences would be like the possible range in miles per hour you may travel.

Method Affects Time

Obviously, changes in method alter the time. Improvements in method should shorten the time. Similarly, the shortcuts used by a skilled man would be recorded on the timestudy as improved methods with corresponding times. Right here is where many supervisors make mistakes in judgment. Too often, they

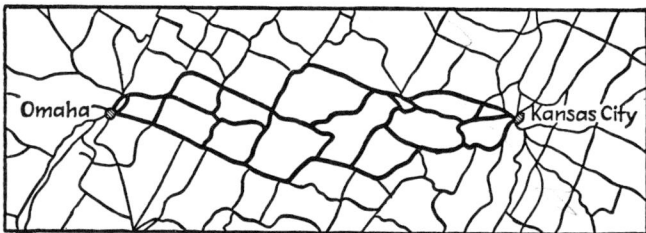

Fig. 6-9. There are many routes you could take in driving from Kansas City to Omaha.

think in terms of total time taken. As a result, they overlook many of the details that make the time of the skilled man so much less than normal.

Differences in skill might be illustrated by comparing an engine lathe with a turret lathe. While both machines do turning, boring, and facing, the engine lathe ordinarily is used for small lots. The turret lathe is assigned the larger quantities. Any one operation that might be done on either machine must be looked at from two points of view.

1. How much longer is the setup time on the turret lathe.
2. How much saving is there in the production time of each.

The added cost of setup for the turret lathe might be thought of as representing a difference in skill. With that assumption, the saving in operation time can be said to result from a difference in method.

Horses and Apples

To make any proper comparison, it is necessary to change things being compared to like terms. In the case of the lathes, it is incorrect to say that one turns out more pieces per hour without considering the loss of production during the difference in setup time.

The difference in setup and in operation would show in good timestudies as unlike elements. The detailed breakdown of an operation records exactly the methods used during the study. Variations in methods used by several people would thus be shown either as different numbers of elements or different elements. The actual times recorded would correspond with the elements performed. However, such studies could not be compared until after they were correctly rated for performance pace and then only so far as the elements were alike. Comparing unrated times or different elements would be as ridiculous as comparing horses with apples.

Describe the Method

Make certain you understand that timestudies can logically be compared only insofar as the elements are alike. It is silly to try to compare unlike things. Hence, good timestudy must separate the method or skill factor by correct element description and breakdown. Such variations are clearly shown when timestudies contain the proper recordings.

Normal Skill

As already mentioned, some of the method differences are variations in skill. The shop explanation of this term *skill* refers to knowledge and use of shortcuts. Thus, a basic question is, "What is the fair measure of skill that is to be called normal?" This is an important point in the field of job evaluation.

Notice however, that job descriptions define skills in words. These are not very helpful to the timestudy man. Yet, he must attempt to set standards that represent the skills required of a normal qualified employee. This he does by recognizing the elements of work repeated in his many studies. In this way, he supplies time measures of the skills specified in job evaluation.

The elements established fix the methods to be used in setting the job standards. These methods should be explained to the employees. Those people with better than normal skill will save some time. They will reduce or eliminate some of the standard elements. Their production will be higher, and it will appear that their efforts are greater.

Fair Day's Work

With method and pace being mixed together, you must know how they alter time and output. Because an operator makes more or less than a standard production does not prove anything with regard to the fairness of the standard. He may not be able to make the standard, and it may be entirely fair. On the other hand, he may "make out" and still have a standard that is too tight.

Therefore, you should remember that regardless of the performance observed, the timestudy man's job is to set fair standards for the elements of work that should be done. The fairness of these standards cannot be judged from either past performance or overall clock times.

Criticizing Standards

Failure to meet the standard rarely results from arithmetical errors in the time allowance. To be sure, errors are made. But the occasional error of a few percent is small in comparison with the more likely difference between a good and a poor performance or method. When 60 minutes an hour (100 percent) is the standard and a man performs at the rate of 50 minutes an hour, the drop is from 100 to 83 percent. This loss of 17 percent is several times the clerical error that might be made in setting the standard. Therefore, when someone says that the standard is "too tight," the first place to look for the difficulty should not be in the standard setting process. Look to see if the pace is right. If this is good, then observe the method being used. Either of these can make major changes in rate of output.

Training in Rating

No one, foreman, manager, union representative, or anyone else who has not been well trained in rating pace can make any worthwhile comments about the fairness of a timestudy standard. Only men having had considerable training in rating are able to judge whether or not a standard is fair. They can do so then only when they see the performance during a correctly taken timestudy.

Timestudy training should be given to the foreman to teach him the need for correctly judging the rate of working and its relation to the actual time taken. Until he has had this training, he is not qualified to judge whether or not an employee is working at a normal pace. It is folly to permit a foreman to take an overall timing when he has not been thoroughly trained to rate the actual performance. Actual stopwatch times that are not corrected by a rating factor will serve only to aggravate an argument.

Looked at from the opposite viewpoint, the foreman who has been thoroughly trained in timestudy methods will be able to judge properly whether or not an operator is trying. He will know that the method being used should conform with the one allowed for in the standard. Probably, he will discover the cause for failure to meet the standard without having to use a stopwatch.

CHAPTER SEVEN

How to Set Consistent Element Times

"Here Joe, you mike it. See what you get." Figure 7-1. You've heard that request more than once if you have worked around machine shops.

Why does one mechanic ask another to mike a dimension? Because several men will get different readings with the same "mike." We say, "They must rely on the 'feel.'" That is why ratchets are attached to some micrometers. Ratchets help to make the readings more consistent.

Judgment Factor

The difference between "mike" readings made by trained men are in their judgments. Judgment is a human quality. It is a variable. Therefore, you would expect to get different answers from several men. The same is true in timestudy. There will be

Fig. 7-1. With quite positive measuring devices like micrometers, shop men do get different answers.

different answers obtained from several timestudies of the same job.

Variations in Timestudies

Variations will show up when you compare several studies. These differences will occur for any one or all of the five reasons.

1. Variations in judging the operator rating.
2. Variations in the element watch reading points.
3. Variations in the methods used by the employee.
4. Variations in the dimensions of the work.
5. Variations in the work conditions of the job.

These variations combine to cause unlike times. Such differences can be seen even on a single timestudy. The example in

Different Normal times for the SAME Element

START __ 2:38 __ RATE __ 75 ____

Element											
Pick up piece			5	06	07	05	05	06	08	05	06
Place in fixture			10	11	13	10	12	11	12	10	16	09
Tighten fixture			08	06	07	09	08	08	09	11	10	08
Start mach.			03	04	04	03	03	05	03	04	03	03
Run to cutter	07		08	09	06	07	07	06	07	08	07	06
Lock feed	03		02	03	03	02	04	03	03	02	03	03
Mill slot	40		40	38	39	40	40	39	41	42	40	43
Run back	10		10	12	10	09	11	10	09	11	08	10
Index fixture	08		09	09	07	08	10	08	08	08	07	06
Run to cutter	09		10	09	11	10	08	09	08	07	07	09
Lock feed	03		03	03	02	03	03	02	03	04	03	03
Mill slot	42		38	42	41	40	43	42	45	41	43	42
Run back	09		09	09	12	08	11	10	08	07	09	10
Index fixture	07		09	06	08	07	07	07	06	07	08	08
Run to cutter	08		08	09	07	08	08	08	08	07	08	07
Lock feed	04		04	03	04	03	04	04	04	03	04	03
Mill slot	43		40	41	43	41	42	44	42	45	43	44
Run back	07		10	07	09	08	06	07	06	07	08	07
Index fixture	09		08	07	09	10	09	06	08	09	09	07
Run to cutter	10		12	10	08	09	10	11	10	09	07	10
Lock feed	03		03	04	03	03	04	04	03	03	04	03
Mill slot	38		38	36	39	37	38	37	39	36	38	40
Run back	08		09	07	08	08	06	10	08	11	07	08
Stop mach.			04	03	03	04	02	04	03	03	04	03
Loosen fixture			07	06	07	05	07	06	06	06	07	06
Remove piece			04	05	05	06	04	06	06	05	05	05
Piece aside			03	04	04	04	04	03	05	03	03	04
Gauge			14				18					

STOP ___ 3:10 _____

It is POOR Timestudy practice to select

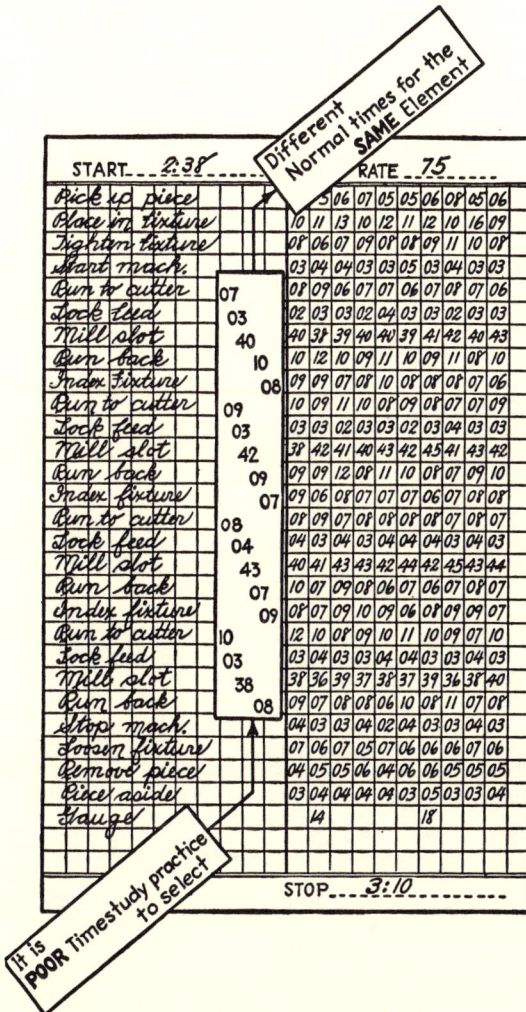

Fig. 7-2. Like elements on one study certainly should have the same selected times.

Figure 7-2 should indicate clearly what is meant. The illustration was selected because it includes repeating elements. For each of the occurrences, a representative time was selected as follows.

Run to Cutter	Run Back	Index Fixture
.07	.10	.08
.09	.09	.07
.08	.07	.09
.10	.08	

You will agree, I'm sure, that the same time should apply to every like element. Hence one selection should have been made from all the watch readings for the same element when conditions were identical. For instance, the fair time for Run to Cutter should have been selected from the 40 readings shown on the study. This example should help you understand why differing element times can occur when many timestudies are taken.

Accuracy versus Consistency

Such variations must be considered when analyzing any group of timestudies taken for building standard data. They will affect the times recorded and the final standards. Errors caused by incorrect judgments and variations in conditions may offset each other. They may all be in one direction, either high or low. These are reasons why it is silly to claim that timestudy standards are accurate. Accuracy comes only with mathematical perfection. The greater the accuracy, the less judgment is permitted to influence the result. But consistency is something entirely different. Consistency in work measurement is the major concern of the timestudy man.

Consistency Is Vital

Inconsistencies in time standards can be seen by anyone. It is the cause of most discussions involving work standards. Usually, the inquiry starts with, "Why don't I get the same for these two jobs? They're just alike." Figure 7-3.

We used this same basic question in Chapter 4. There I wanted to call attention to differences in jobs. Also, I tried to show why two similar operations could have different standards. The stress was placed on unlike work required.

Here we are talking about work standards that should be the same. In this stage, we are highlighting the importance of consistency.

Fig. 7-3. Similar jobs may have different numbers and kinds of elements of work.

Basic Trouble

"It is not the amount but the difference that causes trouble." That is what Harold Bergen used to say. He was referring to differences in base rates. But the same thing holds true with time standards.

The amount is not the most important factor. It is what one man gets in comparison with another that really counts. In timestudy, it is the consistency among standards that is so necessary. *Consistency is more vital than accuracy.* Therefore, an exploration of timestudy comes to a parting of the ways at this point.

The reason is that there are two general methods of setting standard times. One method adds together the element standard times in one study to set one "rate," as explained in Chapter 3.

Two Added Steps

The other method to be described in this book, adds two other steps. These are to gain consistency in the times set for work standards. In addition, this method provides data for compiling standards for operations that were not studied.

You will see these two steps in Figure 7-4, headed "Timestudy Steps." This pictures somewhat the same steps you read in Chapter 3.

First added step. Notice how several timestudies flow together for recording on a Comparison Sheet.

Second added step. Observe that standards for constant and variable elements are set to make up working data before standards are determined for specific jobs.

Timestudy Steps

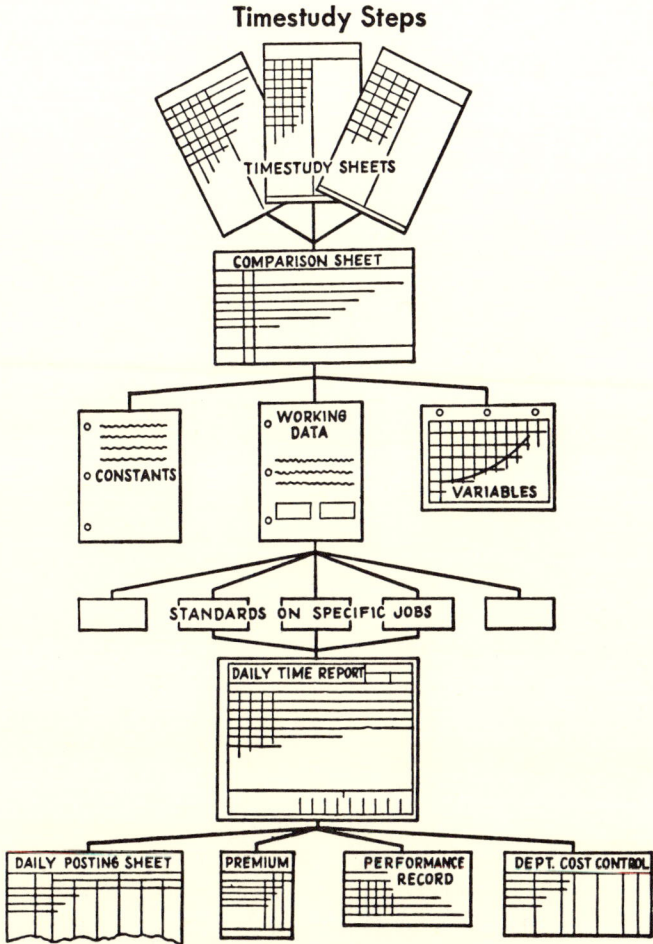

Fig. 7-4. The standard data method adds two steps to gain consistency: (a) a sheet for comparing many studies and (b) determination of data for constants and variables.

One Master Study

Similar consistency could be gained if all standards could be set from one timestudy. But that cannot be done when there are many kinds of pieces being worked on. There are too many differences among jobs. Also, there are numerous elements that are done in some operations that do not occur in others. Moreover, one timestudy would not be sufficient because there would be no check on its correctness. On a single timestudy, each of the element standards might be somewhat in error. Further, future method improvements that eliminated certain elements could leave errors in the remaining totals.

Standard Data Approach

Still, the same thing as "one master study" can be obtained in another way. This is done by fitting together a number of timestudies. The method is used where similar operations are carried on under much the same conditions. A simple example might be the work done on drill presses. Drill press studies would contain many of the same constant and variable elements.

Admittedly, the times allowed for identical constant elements should be exactly the same. Those allowed for the variable elements should be in proper ratio to similar element times. Such consistency can be attained most practically by comparing the elements of a number of timestudies taken of similar operations.

Comparing Timestudies

As you might expect, elements may occur in different sequences in similar operations. Yet, these can be related by

COMPARISON SHEET

STUDY NUMBER		291	304	305	308	315	322
PART NUMBER		15441	19312	17011	25236	24112	14545
MATERIAL		CRS	CRS	CRS	CRS	CRS	CRS
OPERATOR		Bowen	Smith	Block	Jones	Strong	Brown
HOLE-DIA.X DEPTH		1x1½	1½x1½	1¼x1	1x1¾	¾x¾	1¼x¾
WEIGHT-POUNDS		20	35	30	40	3	16
RATING	STAND.	70	80	65	40	65	55
PICK UP PIECE	CURVE1	.09	.15	.11	.19	.04	.07
PIECE ASIDE	CURVE2	.06	.12	.10	.14	.03	.05
LOAD IN JIG	TABLE3	.08	.10	.09	.12	.04	.06
UNLOAD JIG	TABLE3	.06	.08	.07	.10	.03	.04
SPINDLE UP	.03	.03	.02	.03	.03	.04	.03
SPINDLE DOWN	.04	.03	.04	.04	.03	.04	.02

Fig. 7-5. Comparison sheet serves as "one master study" for relating element times from many timestudies.

using a Comparison Sheet like Figure 7-5. Such a recap can be made on any large sheet of paper. The big sheet is arranged so that a number of studies can be recorded on it.

A number of vertical columns are needed. The first of these on the left is a wide one for listing the element descriptions. Here, each description is written, one to a line. No particular order need be followed. However, if there is some rhyme or reason to the sequence of elements, it will be easier to post the timestudy standards. Certainly, the elements should be those obtained by correct detailed breakdowns.

The other columns are ½ inch wide. Each one is for recording the element standards from one study. On a stock form sheet available (1127 Goldsmith), there are 26 such columns.

Recording Conditions

At the top of each study column, the working conditions are noted. These affect the times recorded below. The conditions are referred to when comparing the element times with those of other studies. They are essential in analyzing the differences in element standards.

While some of the studies to be compared may be duplicates, others will be of differing operations. Therefore, it would be expected that some of the element times will be quite different. Consequently, the details posted in the headings at the tops of all columns are very important in the analyses and comparisons of the element times. They are the factors that control the variations.

Amount of Detail

The completeness of the details posted at the tops of the studies has a bearing on the efficiency of the Comparison Sheet. Much time can be lost if the lack of certain information makes it necessary to continually "paw over the studies" themselves. Among the details considered necessary are

Operator's name	Material
Performance rating	Part number
Study number	Equipment type
Size of product	Tools and jigs
Work tolerances	Speed-feed
Quality of finish	Stock removed

Some details that are nonessential under some circumstances might include

Date	Machine number
Observer	Part name
Operator's number	Order number

Rating Is a Variable

Note performance rating is included as an essential detail. Rating should be recognized as one of the variables. It should be recorded to help explain some of the inconsistencies in time standards. This is an important point. It might not seem so to you because, perhaps, you may be in the habit of looking at one study at a time. You should try comparing two studies made of the same operation at different times. Then you will notice that even if working conditions are identical, the times will not be alike. And, with the same or different ratings, there are sure to be variations in element standard times.

1. If other elements show the same percentage difference, the rating is at fault.
2. If an element that precedes or follows the one in question is out of line in the opposite direction, the element breakdown is in error.

Recording Elements

The next step is to record on the Comparison Sheet the element times determined by timestudy. These are the standard times noted in colored pencil on the timestudies. They are posted on the Comparison Sheet in the columns containing the conditions that control, opposite the element descriptions that exactly match those on the timestudies. These element times include relax factors. They were added in the step of converting actuals to normal times (Chapter 6). Hence, these element times are standard times. They are the times that would be used by a "rate setter" to set a "rate" from a single timestudy.

Only standard times should be compared. These element times can be compared because the performance ratings on the timestudies are supposed to have brought all element times to a common normal of work requirement.

Determining Constants

Certain of the elements should be the same. We called these *constants* in Chapter 4. These can be directly compared. Their standard times will vary somewhat. This is to be expected. There are errors in ratings and element breakdowns. However, the variations should be very much less than would be found in the watch readings noted on any one timestudy. Even so, effort should be made to see if the causes of variation can be determined. After all, these standards apply to the same constant elements that are supposed to have identical times.

Investigations should be continued until all the major differences are satisfactorily explained. Then a final standard can be selected for each of the constant elements. This is done in much the same way that one time is set from the several watch readings recorded on one timestudy. These standards are selections, not averages. An average is wrong. It is an arbitrary figure a mathematician can lean on too heavily in proving he is right. A selection is correct because it is the result of analysis and judgment. Thus, one standard is set for each constant element.

These standards are then recorded in the column immediately to the right of the corresponding element descriptions. On the Comparison Sheet, Figure 7-5, one example is Spindle Down .04 minutes. Such standards may later be printed on a

Element	Stand	Occur	Mins
Start and Stop Machine Spindle Up and Down	.06 .07		

Fig. 7-6. Part of a sheet of working data showing combinations of constant element standards.

data sheet in combinations as suggested by the small section shown in Figure 7-6.

Comparing Variable Elements

It is a bit more difficult to compare the standards for the variable elements. The primary reason is that the work itself adds many more differences. Elements that change with the kind of work will vary from one piece to another because of conditions. Several likely variations are brought on by changes in

Size of the work
Rigidity of design
Kind of material
Type of heat treatment
Method of handling
Condition of equipment
Closeness of tolerances
Fineness of finish

Variations in Pieces

In simple words, the variable elements are influenced by dimensional factors. There are differences in sizes of products and of processes. These must be considered in the comparisons that are to be made. The comparisons are most easily made by means of plotted curves. A curve is a convenient form for showing differences in times with corresponding differences in dimensions.

A curve is made up on "squared paper" by using two scales at right angles to each other. The up-and-down scale is laid out in *standard times*. The horizontal scale is marked off in *dimen-*

Pounds Weight	Element Time	Pounds Weight	Element Time
20	.09	3	.04
35	.15	16	.07
30	.11	23	.09
40	.19	10	.05

Fig. 7-7. A few times for variable element Pick Up Piece to be plotted on a curve sheet.

sions like pounds, inches, or square feet. On this paper, the standard times can be compared by plotting. For example, take Pick Up Piece as one of the variables. Assume that the weight of the piece is the controlling factor. On this basis, you will see a few of the standard times from the Comparison Sheet noted in Figure 7-7.

The method of plotting is the same as that so often used in the shop for comparing the results of apparatus performance. For example, the standard time of .09 minutes for 20 pounds is plotted by drawing a small circle (so you can see it) on the line denoting 20 pounds at the point where the time scale equals .09 minutes. Similarly, the standard time of .15 minutes is plotted over the line indicating 35 pounds and opposite the time scale location of .15 minutes. Plotting is started as soon as any variable element standards are set and recorded on the Comparison Sheet. Plotting is continually kept up to date until all the studies have been completed. Then, a final curve or curves are drawn through the plotted points as suggested by Figure 7-8.

Data for Variables

The curves will be representative of the variable elements when enough timestudy results have been plotted. "Enough"

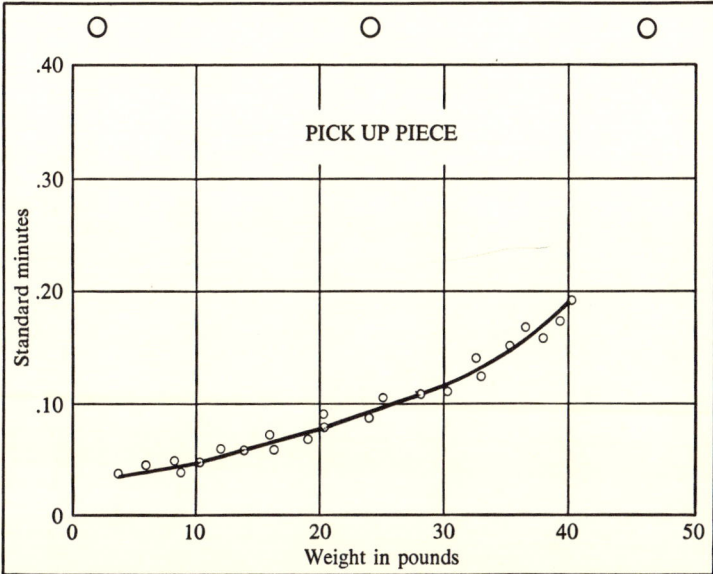

Fig. 7-8. Curve determining standard times for variable element Pick Up Piece.

studies is an important consideration. The timestudies should cover the complete ranges of the variables. But care must be taken, lest there be too many studies made of the average sizes and too few of the extremes. What is necessary are some good studies of a number of sizes all along the range of work.

Number of Studies

How many timestudies should be taken is a question often asked. There is no pat answer. So much depends upon the complexities of the variables. The "rate setter" usually takes one study to set a "rate." He may time a number of pieces. He should stay long enough to convince the operator and the supervisor that he has seen a fair number of pieces made. Strangely, the "rate setter" who decides to use the data method goes from his one study procedure to the opposite extreme. He takes "half a bushel" of timestudies to make up his curves.

A happy medium is more desirable. Enough is enough. Usually, the number of studies taken is reduced when the curve plotting is kept up to date. The important point to remember is that the timestudies must be representative of all the sizes in the range of work. The "sample" must be sufficient to provide fair element standards for the many "sizes" within the range that were not studied. Then, when the curves are drawn through the plotted points, they will provide the correct times for all sizes in that range. When that is assured, then everyone can be certain that all the element standards are fair and consistent with each other.

Element Time Standards

When curves are drawn for all the variables, the difficult part of the comparisons is completed. These curves, together with the constant standards set as described earlier in this chapter, make up a basis for setting operation standards. We call the completed element times *standard data*. Such a basis, in itself, is an assurance of consistency. There are definite standards set to fit defined conditions. These are applied whenever those specified conditions exist. It follows that by using the same element standards for the same conditions, the desired consistency will be obtained.

CHAPTER EIGHT

What Job Details Repeat?

"This job is a new one. You did not time it when you studied the others," said Dave, foreman of the Core Room.

Dave knew what he was talking about. But, what he did not know was that standard data includes times for all elements in a range of work. Dave was like most of us. We do not realize that there are many things different from what we think they are. Usually, that is because we have not learned the whole story. And you, personally, don't want to be caught out on a limb. You want to know the facts about standard data.

What Is Standard Data?

First off, it is possible to set work standards without timing every job. In fact, it is better practice to do so when you use sound standard data. Such a statement may prompt you to ask again, "What is standard data?" The answer is, *"Standard data is the recorded summary of many timestudies."* Usually, it consists of tables, curves, and charts built up from element standards recorded on the Comparison Sheet.

The element standards were obtained by using the "one big timestudy" described in Chapter 7. As a result, we have standards for all the elements likely to occur within the range until there is an important change in method. Changes will take place. Therefore data is never finished. Still, when many timestudies are compared and grouped, standards can be set from that data.

"Builder, Jr."

The simplicity of the standard data method may surprise you. The surprise is that your operations are different only in their combinations of elements. Your department may turn out some products that appear quite unlike others made by a nearby department. Yet, the elements of work may be very similar. These contrasting possibilities may be illustrated by an example. Think of the erector set given to Junior at Christmastime. With this, he can build all sorts of models as suggested by the steam shovel in Figure 8-1. Some he calls "machines." Others are structures like bridges. The "products" he makes vary through the entire range of his imagination.

Even so, the "elements" he uses to build them are all in the one set. They are the metal bars, pulleys, shafts, and assorted bolts that he assembles to suit his project. These parts are like the elements of shop operations.

Elements of a Trade

The elements of standard data are the same work motions that we include when thinking of a particular trade skill. For exam-

Fig. 8-1. Many different products may be made with identical elements in various combinations.

ple, all the elements performed by the "lathe hand" would be recorded in "lathe standard data." When data is completed over the range of work, a standard can be set with it for any work done within that range. The operation standard would be obtained by selecting the proper element times and adding them together.

From this brief explanation you can see how standards can be set without timing each job. But let's go further. What are some of the advantages?

First is *consistency*. You are sure to gain consistency when you use the same standards for like elements that repeat in the "trade."

Second is *speed*. Think how much quicker you can set operation standards when you have all of the element data.

Third is *understanding*. You can explain data standards

more surely and also the revisions that are made necessary by progress.

Fourth is *confidence*. You and your men have confidence in standard data because it is recorded time data.

Reducing Mystery

Standard data is helpful to you because it is much easier to explain. The primary reason is that "standard times" are recorded. They can be referred to in the same way that you look up in a handbook certain information you must have. Being able to do this gets rid of much of the so-called "mystery" about timestudy. Really, it is not mysterious. Actually, it is quite simple to understand. It seems complicated to some people only because

1. They think that only "engineers" are expected to know about timestudy.
2. They have not interested themselves enough to learn how standards are set.
3. They fail to recognize the advantages to them of fair work measurement.

Using Standard Data

You are not to conclude from what has been stated that standard data is a cure-all. It is not. It is simply a method for gaining consistency and economy in setting time standards. It is a very efficient method. It is easy to understand. And, because the standard times are recorded and used each time the elements repeat, many arguments are avoided.

Arguments frequently lead to "horse trading" and compromise. Compromise is sure to produce inconsistency. Standards get out of line with work done. Unfairness results. Dissatisfaction from these causes can be avoided. They can be almost entirely eliminated by

1. Setting consistent operation standards by means of standard data.
2. Explaining to the employees how their operation standards are being set.
3. Seeing to it that operating conditions are kept in line with time allowed.

Use of Data

The practical use of standard data should be readily apparent. In principle, it means that the recorded standard time is allowed for the same element each time it occurs. In two similar jobs, the times allowed for variable elements are similar. They are determined from the same curves or tables that take into account the differences in piece sizes or process dimensions. The same time would be allowed for two variable elements when conditions are alike. This way of setting consistent standard times is fair to all employees. It avoids feelings of discrimination. And remember, it is easy to understand and to explain.

Work Measures

Then, there is the factor of economy. To begin with, you are vitally interested in having all of your work measured. So are your men. They like to know "how they are doin'." And standard data fits this requirement very well. It reduces delay in getting operation standards because timestudy men can set them much more rapidly. In some plants, it requires about one-seventh as long to set a standard from data as by "direct" timestudy.

Standards in Advance

Then too, delay is avoided because standards for new work can be set before the jobs start. They can be set from blueprints. That statement assumes the new work to be within the range of the available data. Also, it assumes that the methods of manufacture are known beforehand.

In contrast, if "rates" are being set by direct timestudy, then the job must be started before it can be timed. This causes delay. It also means that some part of the work is being done without standards. When that happens, your costs go up, your production down. Therefore, one of the advantages of data is that standards can be set to cover practically all work, old and new.

Forms of Standard Data

From the foregoing, you can think of many reasons why standard data is easier for you to work with. Just the same, you should equip yourself to answer all the usual questions about timestudy. You cannot afford to be mystified yourself. If you are, you cannot gain the respect of your people.

With that, let's go on and answer the question, "How can you set a standard without taking a timestudy?" To get started, please take another look at the Comparison Sheet shown in the previous chapter in Figure 7-5. There you will see the notes in the Standard column of Curve 1, Curve 2, Table 3, and constants .03 and .04 minutes. These several notes indicate the forms the data is going to take. Three commonly used forms are

1. Lists of element standard times.
2. Curves of variable element times.
3. Charts and tables of time combinations.

Flow Diagram

Now study the road map called "Timestudy Steps" shown in the previous chapter in Figure 7-4. Notice how the timestudies flow through the Comparison Sheet to become constants and variables. These two kinds of elements can be converted to *Working Data.*

So our next step is to explain how we go from the Comparison Sheet into the Working Data. First, we will take the simplest case. This is to make up a list of constants.

Listed Constants

Sometimes, the standards obtained from the Comparison Sheet are listed for use in setting operation standards. This is done especially when most of the elements are constants. The list is made up by copying the two left-hand colunms of the Comparison Sheet. These are

Element description
Element standard time

These would be arranged in the most convenient order for everyday use. In final form, the list is suitable for setting standards. All that is required is knowledge of the elements necessary to complete the operation and their total numbers. A brief study of the example in Figure 8-2 will indicate one way this may be done. Of course, if the same constants applied to all jobs or to certain groups of operations, they would be

DRILL PRESS—HANDLING TIME	ELEMENT STAND.	NUMBER ALLOWED	STANDARD MINUTES
Tool In and Out—Magic Chuck	.10		
Tool In and Out—Jacob's Chuck	.45		
Change Socket In and Out of Spindle	.38		
Bushings In and Out, up to 1½ in.	.10		
Spindle Up and Down—Drill	.07		
Spindle Up and Down—Cutter, Reamer or Tap	.10		
Move Fixture Between Spindles, under 8 lb.	.04		
Move Fixture Under or Between Spindles 8 to 25 lb.	.06		
Move Fixture Under or Between Spindles 25 to 35 lb.	.10		
Change Speed—Front Head	.10		
Start and Stop Machine	.06		
Lubricate Tool or Hole by Brush	.03		

Equals .03 +.04

Fig. 8-2. For ease in standard setting, constant elements are combined. See Spindle Up .03 and Spindle Down .04 on Comparison Sheet, Chapter 7.

added before listing. Combining is illustrated by the total of .07 minutes for Spindle Up and Down.

Grouped Constants

The same method is used for groups of elements that always occur together. But, whether elements are listed singly or as totals of grouped elements, the standard is set by selecting those that apply. For instance, figures written in the column Number Allowed show how often each element is to be done. Then, these figures are multiplied by the standard shown in the column labeled Element Standard. The total amount allowed for each element is noted in the column headed Standard Minutes. In this way, all constant elements are considered and the total computed for the operation.

Charted Constants

When a lot of multiplying is necessary to set standards, a chart can save clerical work. An example is Figure 8-3, made up for

Number of times.............	1	2	3	4	5
Caliper dimension.............	.03	.06	.09	.12	.15

Fig. 8-3. Charts of multiplied constants save repeated clerical work.

Gauge 1 in every.............	1	2	3	4	5
Micrometer	.12	.06	.04	.03	.02

Fig. 8-4. Charts should be made of prorated elements to save repeated calculating.

multiples of calipering. This element was a major portion of a rough castings inspection operation.

This multiplying procedure is often reversed. The idea is a good one. We make more mistakes in dividing than in multiplying. One example is gauging. In production, it is usually required that the operator measure one in so many. For this purpose, the varying number between gaugings was divided into the standard for Gauge One. A chart of the standard times resembles that shown in Figure 8-4.

Curves of Variable Elements

Constant elements are comparatively simple to chart. In contrast, variable elements have many standards for one element description. The reason is that some factor like length or weight influences the time. The standard time is greater, in the next example, when the weight is heavier. This is illustrated by the curve in Figure 8-5 shown for Piece Handling. The curve was drawn to represent the standard times found by combining two elements. Comparison Sheet standards for Pick Up Piece and Piece Aside shown in Chapter 7 were added together to obtain the totals plotted. These sums are shown as

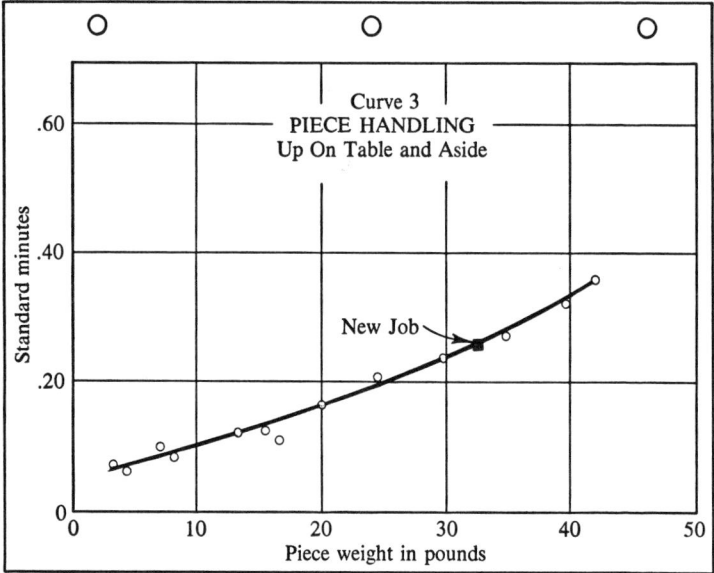

Fig. 8-5. The arrow points to a Piece Handling standard time for a job that was not studied.

the small circles drawn over the weights and opposite the standard times.

If this curve seems a little mysterious to you, don't let it "get you down." Instead, review how curves are plotted as explained in Chapter 7. You should make sure that you understand what a curve really is.

The curve is not complicated. It is the most common method for showing the relation of time to some dimensional factor. And it is used by all well-trained timestudy men to get the standards for variable elements.

Reading Curves

Now, to read the curve in Figure 8-5, let's take the example of a 32 pound job. The correct standard time for it is .24 minute.

This standard, read from the curve, is consistently fair. That is because the line was drawn to fairly represent all the jobs studied.

Not every job is studied. There are at least three reasons.

1. Jobs studied are representative of the range of work then existing.
2. Some weights did not exist in the plant when the studies were taken.
3. Certain jobs were not running during the period of time-study observations.

These three points bring out one chief reason why standard data is advantageous. They emphasize the fact that with a representative "sample" of jobs, curves can be drawn without studying all jobs. This will become apparent to you if you study the line with respect to the points. This final line gradually increases the time allowed as the weight goes up. Hence, *standard minutes* allowed are fair for any weight along the line. That brings us to the important conclusion that

> *A fair standard can be set from data for any operation that falls within the range studied.*

Curves to Tables

At this point, let's assume that you understand curves. They represent element time standards that vary with changes in dimensions of the product or the process. Maybe both.

Looking closely at the curve in Figure 8-5, you can see that you could "read off" an infinite number of standard times. Note also that you could make mistakes in your readings. Besides, curve reading is slow—hence costly.

To avoid these problems, we take the next step. We convert the curves to tables of definite numbers. However, you do not want to get lost by the change in looks. The curve and the table made from it are simply two forms of the same basic data. But numbers shown in a table are

Easier to read	Faster to use
Simpler to explain	Surer to apply

Charts and Tables

For the reasons given, tables and charts are used mostly to record variable element times. They replace curves because they are surer and faster to work with. They are made up by taking selected readings from the curves. First, the desired dimensions are listed. Then, the corresponding standard times are read from the curve or curves. The dimensions may be selected for specific conditions. Generally, they are taken over the whole range of the curve.

The spacings may be uniform like 5, 10, 15, . . . , 50. Another way is to read the curves at percentage time intervals like each 10 percent. I prefer time percentage intervals.

Whatever method is used, a relatively few standards will be selected instead of many curve readings. The smaller number is better for all practical purposes. Almost no errors are introduced. And considerable time and space are saved.

More to the point, you can understand a table with less effort. So can your people. But remember you need to

1. Be able to explain how a curve is made of a variable element.
2. Be able to see the curve behind a table of standards read from it.

Working Data

The previous simple examples were chosen to make standard data more understandable to you. You should know, however,

that most standards must be set for more complicated operations. The usual standard involves both constants and variables. The job of standard setting is the same except that more
factors must be considered. More time is required to set the
standard. It is here that the form of the data begins to show
its importance.

As the data becomes more complex, the several forms are
combined into what I call "working data." This often utilizes
tables made from curves of variables, together with charts and
lists of constants. An example is the portion of a sheet of drill
press data illustrated in Figure 8-6. Observe the table near the
top of the chart. There you see five variable elements arranged
by weight. In the lower table, you see the Jig Handling times
recorded by jig size.

To set a standard with this sheet, you simply record the
number of times beside each of the necessary elements. Note
the word "necessary." A correct standard allows for only the
elements of work that are required. Then you multiply and
post the answers in the Standard Minutes column. Finally, you
add all your extensions to obtain the operation standard.

UPRIGHT DRILL PRESS										
Material_____ Operation_____ Part Number_____										
Piece Wt._____ Part Name_____										
Jig Wt._____ Jig Class_____ Date_____										
Total_____ Jig Holding_____ Set by_____										
	Piece or Combined Weight								NUMBER	STANDARD MINUTES
	1	6	11	19	28	40	54	60		
Piece Up, On, Off, Aside......	06	08	13	22	30	43	69	80		
Move To, or Hole-Hole.......	02	02	02	03	03	03	04	04		
Turn or Index 90 deg........	02	02	03	03	04	04	05	05		
Turn or Index 180 deg........	03	04	05	05	06	07	08	08		
Blow Chips.	04	04	05	06	07	09	10	12		
	Jig Lid Size									
	3 x 3	3 x 5	4 x 6	5 x 8						
Close and Open Lid, ¼ Turn Screw......	06	10	12	16						
T and L (1) Wing, Thumb, Screw........	08	11	13	15						
T and L ¼ Turn Clamp................	08	11	13	15						
T and L (2) Wing, Thumb Screws........	10	12	15	19						
T and L (1) Socket Head Screw.....	20	23	26	30						

Fig. 8-6. Part of a sheet of working data for drill press operations.

Explaining Revisions

As you have just learned, standards are set by

1. Selecting the elements required.
2. Multiplying these by occurrences.
3. Adding the extensions to get the total.

Suppose now there is, as there will continue to be, a method improvement. Assume that this eliminates some elements. Then you have two choices. One is to revise the standard if you are already set for the operation.

The other, and I think better, choice is to set a new standard for the work required under the new conditions. This is the logical approach. Besides, it avoids errors of inflation that could occur if the prior standard had in it any excess time.

Knowing Data Forms

These descriptions and examples of data forms are very brief. But you should gain from them a basic understanding of the several ways of setting up standard data. Perhaps all different forms will be used by the Timestudy Department in your plant. For that reason, it is important that you know how to read and use all of them. It would be simpler if only one form were used throughout. But each has its particular use just like the tools in the shop. That point may be obvious to you. It is stated, however, to assure you that the timestudy man does not use several different forms of standard data for the fun of it.

Perhaps the timestudy man himself does not know that he could improve upon his method of setting up standard time data. Maybe you can suggest to him how he can make it simpler and more understandable.

Better Attitude

The purpose of this explanation is to emphasize the value to you of being able to see how the standards can be determined from standard data. With that knowledge, you are in a much better position to answer the questions of your people. Remember that work performances depend upon the right combinations of working conditions, skills, and attitudes. The attitude is the major factor. It is affected considerably by the confidence the operators have in their standards.

Here is where you can be of so much help to yourself and to your department. You can bring about the right attitude by learning to answer correctly the questions asked about standards and timestudy. This requires an understanding of curves, charts, and tables. Therefore, it is to your advantage to make sure that you know enough about each one of these forms of data to make clear explanations to your own group.

You should know for certain that

1. Consistency of standards results from comparing and grouping elements from many timestudies.
2. Fairness of work measurement follows from repeated use of correct element data.
3. Mystery of timestudy vanishes when you explain it with recorded charts and tables.
4. Misunderstandings of preset standards are replaced by insistences upon having that kind.

CHAPTER NINE

How to Set Standards

"Where did you get this standard? Did you allow me time for all the work I have to do in this operation?" asked Bill Jones. Bill's question is a common one. Perhaps he learned about timestudy in a plant where "rates" were set only from single studies.

The Usual Notion

Bill asks his question for at least two reasons. First, we have failed to explain to him how standards can be set from standard data. But also he thinks we do have to time his job. He believes that because his experiences have taught him that standards are set with a stopwatch.

You may have some such questions in your mind. Therefore, you want to know more about setting standards. You must understand that there are two ways to set them. The single study method is more direct and more people know about it.

It was called "rate setting" in Chapter 3. Its simplicity is offset, however, by two basic disadvantages. One is its very high cost. The other, of more concern, is its inconsistent "rates."

These two defects are overcome by using the Standard Data method without complicating the standard setting process. As a matter of fact, it simplifies the problems of "communicating" with the employees. You can much more easily explain standard setting to them. This important part of your job will be described in the next chapter. At this point, the different steps in the two methods might be stated again for review. The several steps are

Single Study	*Standard Data*
Element breakdown	Element breakdown
Rating performance	Rating performance
Applying relax	Applying relax
	Plotting variable elements
	Comparing element times
	Recording element data
Setting element times	Setting element standards
	Selecting required elements
Adding element times	Adding element standards

First Added Step

The step listed as comparing element times in the previous paragraph can be taken two ways. It could mean comparing the several stopwatch times for an element on a single study. That is done in the "rate setting" method to set element times.

Here, we mean something entirely different. In the data method, this first step refers to the use of the Comparison Sheet for comparing element times. You will recall that standards for constants were selected from element times on the Comparison Sheet. You will remember that the variable element times were plotted for comparison and analysis. The resulting standards are more representative of normal performance—"a fair day's work."

Second Added Step

Since we developed element standards from the Comparison Sheet, we have to add another step. This involves determining the elements to be allowed in the work standard. Observe that those elements recorded on the timestudies may or may not be the ones required to do the job. Remember, the highly skilled man may use some shortcuts.

Regardless, the combinations of elements observed in timestudies are disregarded when we build data for a *type of work*. In the standard data method, we are setting standards for all the elements in all the jobs of a type. Let me repeat. We are setting standards for all the elements the "lathe hand," for example, is likely to use in doing all of his operations. These are the job details that repeat in operations done by men in a "trade."

Extra Work

In addition to the regular elements, extra work is sometimes done. Usually this is caused by faulty conditions. For instance, the material may be too hard or too soft, too thick or too thin. Such conditions the foreman must try to control. But when extra work is done, it shows on the timestudies as added elements or longer elements. In either case, it is extremely important that the timestudy man record and analyze these extras. I say, "It is more necessary to record the extras than the regular elements." We can study the regular elements any time. But data for the irregular elements is necessary because those elements will occur again. When they do, either we set extra allowance standards or "let the job go daywork."

Selecting the Elements

When the data is completed, the second added step is to get together the elements required for specific jobs. This step is called *standard setting*. It is done by means of a Working Data Sheet such as you will see illustrated in Figure 9-1. The process

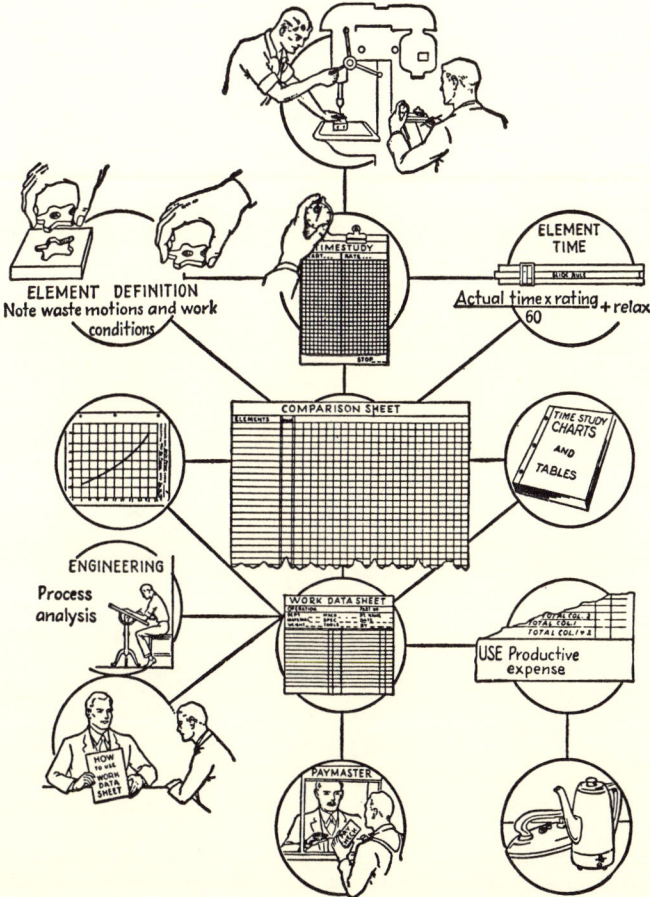

ELEMENT DEFINITION
Note waste motions and work conditions

TIMESTUDY

ELEMENT TIME

$$\frac{\text{Actual time} \times \text{rating}}{60} + \text{relax}$$

COMPARISON SHEET

TIME STUDY CHARTS AND TABLES

ENGINEERING
Process analysis

WORK DATA SHEET

USE Productive expense

PAYMASTER

Fig. 9-1. A pictorial illustration of the several steps in the standard data method of timestudy.

is somewhat like selecting the parts from the stockroom to make up an assembly as suggested by Figure 9-2. Only certain pieces are needed. Neither more nor less will assemble correctly.

So it is with standard setting. It is important to allow the right elements. Unfortunately, the element standard times can be added even if they are selected or multiplied incorrectly. In this step lies one of the mistakes the "rate setter" may make.

Fig. 9-2. Selecting the elements that go to make up an operation standard time is similar to selecting parts from the storeroom for an assembly.

His single study shows the elements that were done. These may not be the ones that should be done.

Including Correct Elements

With standard data, there is more control over correct element inclusion. One factor is that the elements established from many timestudies more properly represent fair measures of normal skill. A second aid is in element groupings. These will be described later in this chapter. At this stage, you should realize that the correctness of the operation standard depends upon doing correctly four functions.

1. Allowing for all necessary elements.
2. Disregarding times for extra work.
3. Selecting the correct element times.
4. Extending and adding the standard times.

Necessary Elements

The operator must be allowed time for all necessary work. This may call for two standards. One is for extra work he may have to do. The other is for the regular operation. Our concern here is with setting standards for the productive operations. Hence, our next step is to find out what should be done. This may be as obvious as the assembly of parts just illustrated. More often, some detailed information must be obtained. In some cases, the missing details may be gotten by making a check of the operation itself. Practically, the same thing is done. The timestudy man who knows the work uses his experiences to determine the necessary elements. The experienced man may have worked in the shop on the actual operations. His knowledge of the work enables him to select the correct elements in most cases.

Patterns of Work

Many times the standard setter is aided by element groupings. This gain can be utilized in many kinds of operations because there are *patterns of work*. The groupings follow the principle stated by Frederick W. Taylor as, "Add together into various groups such combinations of elementary motions as are frequently used in the same sequence in the trade. . . ." One common example in lathe operations is

Pick Up Piece	Loosen Tailstock
Set in Centers	Remove Piece
Tighten Tailstock	Piece Aside

There are many such "patterns" in manufacturing operations. To the extent they do exist, groupings

1. Save decision making and clerical work.
2. Reduce chances of errors in selections.
3. Standardize elements allowed in jobs.

Correct Element Standards

Even with groupings, it is sometimes necessary for the timestudy man to get certain details that are not known to him. He may go to the shop or to the "blueprint" for the details he needs. These are principally related to the variables. For instance, he may have to find out how much a part weighs. Or, he may need to learn what kind of a jig or fixture is to be used. Such information about variables is needed because there are several standard times for each one. The right one must be selected and allowed. Briefly, this describes the selecting of the proper elements. The rest of the standard setting process is largely clerical. It involves extending, adding, and recording.

Charted Element Data

Going on, let's tackle the setting of some standards. We can start with a simple one. An example that is easy to understand is one that measures the inspection of rough castings. The times apply to castings weighing between 2 and 7 pounds. The chart of data is shown in Figure 9-3. The standard setting in this case is fairly easy. First, you must know what elements of work are to be done in inspecting the piece.

Notice that Pick Up Piece and Piece Aside are done once to each piece. So the quantity 1 and its extension are printed on the data sheet. Then comes the question of how many times each of the other elements is repeated. The answers to this question for a particular casting are noted as the handwritten figures in the Number of Times column. These quantities are the multipliers for extending the element times. Each is multiplied by the standard for the element (caliper dimension .03 × 3 =.09). The results are written in the Allowed column. Then, the addition of all extensions gives the total of .24 standard minute for the operation.

Rough Casting Inspection	Standard Mins.	Number Times	Allowed
Pick Up and Aside...	.03	1	.03
Ring for Sound......	.02	1	.02
Test Straightness....	.02	2	.04
Caliper Dimension...	.03	3	.09
Visual Inspect.......	.02	3	.06
Total.............			.24

Fig. 9-3. Standard data may consist of a simple list of constant elements.

Curves of Variables

Standard setting that involves variable elements is somewhat more complicated. As you will recall, a variable is an element whose time changes by gradual alterations in some conditions. Variables are usually drawn on curves when they are analyzed. Sometimes, the final curves are read and written down on tables. For that reason, we will first set standards from curves.

Data Curves

Two curves are needed to set a standard in this example because the operation consists of Piece Handling and Machining Time. Several elements are included in both curves. For simplicity, only the totals were used to plot the curves. To set a standard, we will start with the Handling Time curve.

Assume the weight of the piece to be 18 pounds. Now, go

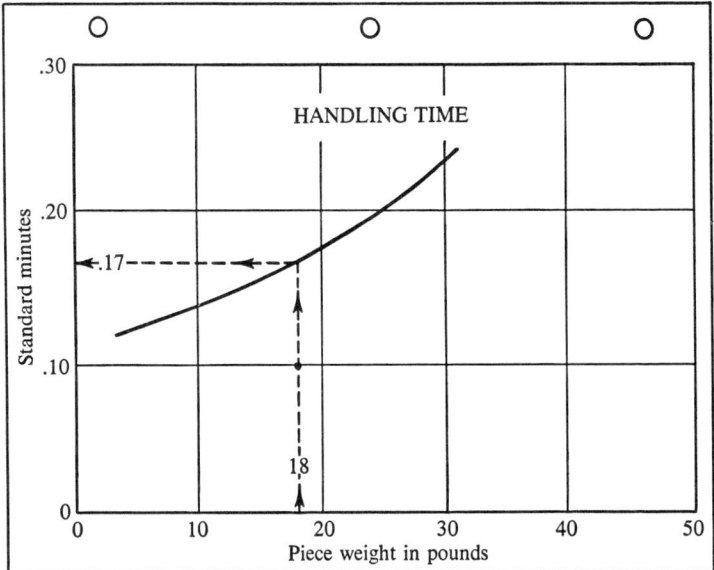

Fig. 9-4. The Handling Time for an 18 pound piece is .17 minute.

out along the bottom of the curve in Figure 9-4 until you come
to 18 pounds. Go vertically along the dotted line until you
come to the curve. Then, turn left and move over to the Time
scale. There you read .17 standard minute. This time is read
from the Standard minutes scale at the place where a horizontal line from the point where the 18 pound vertical line
touches the curve extends to the time scale.

Directions for Reading Handling Time Curve.
1. Locate 18 pounds on the Piece Weight in the pounds scale.
2. Move vertically along the 18 pound line to the curve.
3. Go left from that point on curve to standard minutes scale.
4. Read the time .17 in standard minutes.

Following the same general directions on the Machining
time curve in Figure 9-5, read the time for 2¼-inch diameter
as .36 standard minute.

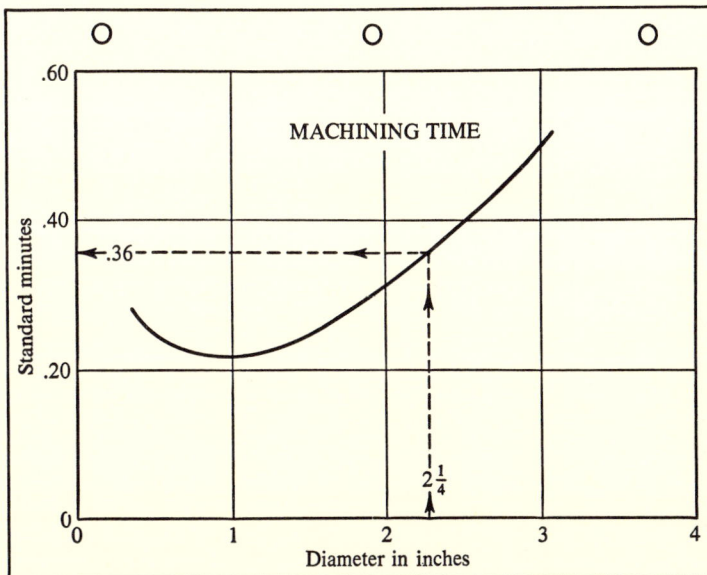

Fig. 9-5. The Machining Time for 2¼-inch diameter is .36 minute.

Part weighs................18 lb.	.17 min.
Diameter..................2¼″	.36 min.
	Total Standard .53 min.

Fig. 9-6. The orderly recording of the two standards shows a total of .53 minute.

Directions for Reading Machining Time Curve.
1. Locate 2¼ inches on the Diameter, Inches scale.
2. Move up along 2¼ inches vertical to the curve.
3. Turn left, go horizontally to the Time scale.
4. Read the time .36 in standard minutes.

Recording the Handling and the Machining curve readings in an orderly way, the total standard of .53 minute would appear something like that shown on the chart in Figure 9-6.

Garden Variety Jobs

Chances are that the jobs in your department have more elements in them than we worked with in the preceding examples. So, let's set a standard for a more usual operation. Drill press work can serve to illustrate. Don't groan. Many have said, "Why pick drill press?" The best reason is that most people know what a drill press is. Many have them in their cellar workshops.

To set a standard, we will take an operation of drilling two holes. Both holes are 1 inch in diameter. One hole is ½ inch deep. The other is ¾ inch deep. The piece weighs 17 pounds. Now, refer to the charts in Figure 9-7. There you find three charts of combined elements. We can read these in any sequence that is convenient. Since they are labeled A, B, C, we will read them in that order. Looking first at Chart A, we find:

MINUTES TO DRILL ONE HOLE

PIECE
HANDLING

A	Drill Diameter			
Deep	½	¾	1	1¼
¼	.06	.09	.12	.15
⅜	.07	.10	.13	.17
½	.08	.11	(.14)	.19
⅝	.09	.12	.16	.21
¾	.11	.14	(.18)	.23
⅞	.13	.16	.20	25
1	.15	.18	.22	.28
1⅛	.17	.20	.25	.31
1¼	.19	.23	.28	.34

Note.—Depth includes Drill Point.

C Wt.	Min.
6.	.08
8	.09
10	.10
12	.11
14	.12
17	(.13)
20	.14
23	.16
26	.18
29	.20
32	22
35	.25

B	ADDITIONAL HANDLING					
Drill Jig Load and Unload Blow Chips		Weight of Piece				
		6–8	10–14	17–23	26–29	32–35
		.16	.19	(.22)	.27	32
R and L Spindle	No. of H o l e s	1	12	13	.14	.15	17
		2	.17	.19	(.21)	.23	.27
Move H-H		3	.22	.25	.28	.31	.37
		4	.29	.31	,35	.39	.47

Fig. 9-7. Standards for drill press that combine many elements into three charts.

CHART A   Under 1-inch diameter, opposite ½ inch deep, circle .14 minute.

Under 1-inch diameter, opposite ¾ inch deep, circle .18 minute.

There are more elements of work. The piece goes in a jig. The loaded jig is moved hole to hole. Therefore, refer to Chart B of Additional Handling.

CHART B   Under 17–23-pound weight find .22 minute for Drill Jig.

Under 17–23-pound weight, opposite 2 holes circle .21 minute for Raise and Lower Spindle, Move Hole to Hole.

CHART C   Opposite the weight of 17 pounds is the standard of .13 minute for Piece Handling.

Common practice is to formally record the makeup of a standard. Hence, on the chart in Figure 9-8, you will see the element descriptions with their standards. The chart references are noted also.

Elements	Minutes	Chart
Pick Up Piece Piece Aside } 17 lb.	.13	*C*
Load and Unload Jig Blow Chips } 17 lb. . . .	.22	*B*
Raise and Lower Spindle } 2 Move Hole-Hole } 2	.21	*B*
Drill 1″ diameter × ½″ deep. .	.14	*A*
1″ diameter × ¾″ deep. .	.18	*A*
Total Standard.	.88	

Fig. 9-8. Table showing the standards selected from the three drill press data charts in Figure 9-7.

Possible Errors

The final data charts such as the ones we have been working with show fair standard times for normal qualified people. They are built up from many studies. But mistakes can occur in using them

1. When the method of manufacture is incorrectly described.
2. When the standard time is taken from the wrong location.
3. When the total of the several standards is added incorrectly.

For instance, you might have circled the .13 minute standard for $3/8$ inch in depth when $3/4$ inch is the correct dimension and .14 minute the correct standard. You might have been absent-minded and used $1/2$ inch in diameter instead of 1 inch and circled .11 minute for $3/4$ inch in depth. However, when you circle a standard, you mark your trail. Thus, you can retrace your steps. You can check your work. You can explain how you got whatever answer you obtained.

So long as no errors are made, all standards set from such tables will be consistent with each other for the work done. Such tables are easy to understand. A brief explanation of the elements included is about all the "communication" necessary. When you know how they were made up, you should be able to tell your people how their standards are set.

Your Job Made Easier

Such charts of standard data are sure to be fairly representative of normal performance. The standards measure a fair day's work because the data was built up from many timestudies taken under shop working conditions. Consequently, any one standard set from the data is as fair as any other. This gives you a very decided advantage. You can sit down with your people and discuss their standards.

As you improve their understandings, you increase their confidence in their work measures. Any differences between work done and time allowed will thus be discovered. These differences usually result from misunderstandings of the methods to be used. If the employee is using the wrong method, he can be corrected. If the standard has not included all the necessary work, it should be made correct. If extra work is necessary because of some faulty condition, an extra allowance should be made. Of course, you want to make every effort to correct the faulty conditions. They lower your production and increase your costs. These variations will be explained more fully in Chapter 10.

Here, we are discussing basic standard setting. I hope that these few examples have been easily understood. You should know how elements of standard data are fitted together to set operation standards. With this general outline in mind, you should be able to set standards from data. When you know how to set standards, you will have more confidence in them. In addition, you can more clearly explain them to your men. You will know that

1. The employees were studied while working on a large variety of operations.
2. The studies were taken at all periods of the working time by several timestudy men.
3. The completed data includes element standards obtained from a large number of timestudies.
4. The standard data is the fairest method for measuring a fair day's work.

CHAPTER 10

Be Sure to Explain Timestudy

"How is a fella supposed to make out when he doesn't know what's in his standard?" That's what Jim asks. He is right. If he does not know what is expected of him, he is in the "dark."

As you know, many things can happen that take more time than is allowed in the work standard. Four should be mentioned.

1. Did you teach him the correct method?
2. Did you tell him the quality to produce?
3. Did you cause him to wait for material?
4. Did you ask him to do some extra work?

Factors like these can greatly affect Jim's attitude and his performance. Besides, you should know what causes his question. Your job and his would be easier if he knew the right answers. Jim might not be so troubled if he correctly understood what was included in his standard. Why not explain to him so he will know how standards are set?

Whose Job Is It?

Many a foreman insists that it is not his job to explain standards and timestudy to his people. Maybe he is right, technically. Actually, however, the responsibility for training his men belongs to the foreman. He should do a good job of instructing his men for at least two reasons.

1. He wants to get quality workmanship on time at low costs.
2. He is looked to by his people for development into better jobs.

Certainly, giving his people the right understanding of work measurement is a practical step toward both aims. Besides, employees are better satisfied when they are able to do their jobs more effectively.

Training Programs

Someone must do the training. Much of it may be taken over by a personnel division in some of the big shops. This is not usually the case. Even if it were, that would not relieve the foreman of his responsibility for answering questions about work standards.

More to the point, the foreman needs the "loyalty" of the individuals in his group. For this reason alone, he must clearly indicate who is foreman. He can do this indirectly by explaining how things are to be done in his department.

The Foreman's Prestige

You can argue that the timestudy man should do the job of explaining. Undoubtedly, he knows more about it because that is his work. Unquestionably, the timestudy man should help. He should clear up whatever technical questions arise as suggested by Figure 10-1. But to say that the timestudy man is responsible for explaining because he knows all the answers is an excuse—not a reason. The foreman who says that would be more correct if he simply said, "I don't want to learn about timestudy."

Either way, the foreman loses out. He loses prestige with his

Fig. 10-1. Do you give me time for gauging these pieces?

people because he appears to be ignorant about work standards. He cannot afford that. It is much too costly for him to lose respect.

Why Explain Standards?

Neglecting to explain standards and timestudy to his employees does not make the foreman's job easier. He may think so. But, the time he thinks he has "saved" is more than wasted later in straightening out complaints. Most of the arguments about standards would disappear if the foreman did this part of his job. Of course, his work is not finished when he does give careful explanations. He must repeat these until the operators' questions are satisfactorily answered.

What Is Involved

Two parts of the explanations that he should give deserve special emphasis. These are

1. Attitude—establishing confidence in the fairness of the work standards.
2. Conditions—explaining conditions allowed for in standards considering method, quality, and lost time.

Both are somewhat like playing a game. For example, not only must you want to play ball, but also you must know the rules.

Start at the Beginning

Many of the Why questions about work standards can be answered by explaining the timestudy procedure until it is un-

derstood. Explain all about element breakdown (rating especially) and relax factors, and how these combine to give
standard data. Then, by using one of his operations to
illustrate, the employee can be shown how each element of
work is allowed for from recorded time values. In fact, probably, the workman could set his own standard after the data
has been properly reviewed with him, as indicated in Figure
10-2. This means

1. Personalities can be left out of the discussions about standard data.
2. Job comparisons can be made in detail and their differences
   justified.
3. Work performance measures are made uniform by the use
   of consistent data.

Fig. 10-2. An employee should be able to set his own standard after the standard data has been thoroughly explained to him.

4. Revisions caused by method changes are readily explained by obvious additions or subtractions.
5. Operation standards can be reproduced if the records become lost accidentally or on purpose.

Method Instruction

The usual workman is more than intelligent enough to understand the details of timestudy. But, he is not a mind reader. He cannot be expected to imagine what method was allowed for in the standard time. Unfairness exists as soon as there is an inconsistency between what is allowed for and what he does. That should be just as obvious as the fact that a dozen is neither 11 nor 13.

The foreman should know better than most people that *one method* is best for the current shop conditions. That method must be known to the producer. He must learn it from a qualified instructor. Usually that instructor is his foreman. This is the best practice. Primarily, the foreman can be consistent in his teaching. He can gain more uniformity in the methods to be followed when he does the teaching. He may be assisted by the use of

| Timestudies | Route cards |
| Instruction cards | Operation sheets |

When good instructions and written details are given, the operator knows what he is supposed to do in the time allowed.

Informing Employees

Hence, your part is twofold. And the purpose of all this explaining is to help you answer the two following questions

Question 1. Is Jim using the method called for in the work standard?

Question 2. Are the working conditions correct for the standard as set?

First, let's talk about method. As soon as we start, you have to think, "Did I tell Jim what method to use? Am I expecting him to be a mind reader?" From such questions you realize that Jim cannot know exactly what the method should be unless you instruct him.

Don't balk now. I know how you feel. You are like every supervisor I know. You say, "For cryin' out loud, why can't I ever get a good mechanic?" I agree with you. But what you mean is, "Why can't I get men who can go ahead without bothering me?"

Timestudy Is Exact

Either way, it's not enough. Timestudy is too exact for such loose methods. Only certain elements are allowed for in the standard. If 12 elements are necessary, the standard does not include 13, 14 or 20 elements. Only 12 are included. Thus, the man who makes extra moves will lose out. And because he is your man, you will have a complaint on your hands. Your man will say, "The standard is tight," as in Figure 10-3.

The standard is not the fault. Maybe what's wrong is that he was not instructed on how to do the job by the standard method. Or perhaps conditions were faulty in some way. So your first concern is to see that Jim knows exactly what work is allowed for in his standard.

Fig. 10-3. The individual who does not know what he is supposed to do is likely to say, "Standard too tight."

Quality Output

The next point of instruction has to do with quality. What is expected in quality workmanship? How does Jim know when he is done with his operation? Note, the question of quality has two sides. One is that the standard covers work for a definite degree of perfection. Jim must know what acceptable work is. If he slights the work, the standard allows too much.

The other is that Jim will be doing extra work if excess quality is demanded. Both sides have to be upheld. And this can be done when the operator knows what is expected of him. Thus, knowledge of what is right and wrong in quality is very important in proper work measurement. You do not want your people turning out a lot of "bum" work at high speed. They must be taught both to meet quality standards and to work effectively. In this respect, you should allow credit for only the work that is up to the level of quality that is specified by the standard time.

Time off Standard

Of course, your people cannot turn out quality products while they "wait." For instance, do they have to stand in line at the tool crib as depicted in Figure 10-4? Time is lost when your work is not planned so that your people can "keep going." Material is delayed. Tools are not ready. Machines break down. These and other delays are under your control. Such irregularities are not included in good timestudy standards. Any attempt

Fig. 10-4. Men can't turn out production while they are waiting for tools.

to allow them would start with an average. And everybody would be quarreling about "above average" delays. A better practice is to give credit for delays as they happen. For this reason, it is part of any complete instruction to emphasize that delays are to be recorded. They are to be reported separately.

Report Delay Times

You may argue that reporting delays is "cutting your own throat." That is true from a narrow-minded point of view. But if you want to be a good foreman you must begin to look at costs in the same way your boss does. The basic question is, "How can anybody tell how much lost time there is if it is buried?"

You should insist that all delay time be reported. You want the increases in production and the reductions in cost you can get by cutting the delay times. In addition, you want to make certain that your people are treated fairly. You know that their performances drop down if you try to hide your own inefficiencies.

Knowing Conditions

Having done first things first, you and Jim instantly recognize when it is not possible to follow the standard method. Road blocks interfere when conditions go wrong.

1. Maybe the previous operation was not done completely or correctly.
2. Maybe the castings have too much stock on them for the number of cuts allowed.

3. Maybe the material is too hard to cut at the feeds and speeds specified.

Extra Work

If there are differences in working conditions, grievances are present. The extras cause more work. This prompts the employee to complain, "The standard is wrong." Then, too often, the foreman simply echoes the bitching to the timestudy man. He "sounds off" without thinking or looking.

Both foreman and employee should understand the conditions underlying the standard. When each knows what has been allowed for in the standard, attention is called to poor materials, tools, and equipment. The producer can help only so far as he knows what is expected. And the foreman must know what work elements are included. When both understand, poor conditions are easily recognized. Then, action can be taken to improve them so that the time allowed is again fair. Or allowances can be made for extra work required.

Added Work

Extra work is made up of added elements. Similar extra elements were stressed a few pages earlier when we discussed incorrect methods. There we pointed out the necessity for training to eliminate extra motions. Such training is for the purpose of

1. Aiding the operator's working capacity by avoiding wasted effort.
2. Guiding the employee in exact knowledge of what the standard includes.

In contrast, when extra work is made necessary by some faulty conditions, then the extra elements should be allowed. However, these extra elements should not be added to the standard. They should be kept separated. Such extra work is *indirect labor*. It is added cost—not more production. It is usually just the same as rework.

Time Taken

Further, times of delays and extra work can affect earnings. This can be true in the many plants that use work standards for wage incentive applications. Incentive earnings are related to "time taken." They are usually determined as the difference between "time taken" and "time allowed." The time allowed is established by standard data, "rate setting," or "guessti-mating."

The time taken is what you must concern yourself about. You want a full day of productive effort as shown on the chart in Figure 10-5. Proper instruction, quality standards, extra work, and wait time become more critical. All these factors enter into the "time taken." The time "on standard" is charged to the jobs or operations done in your shop. It is the time the employees have to increase their earnings. Naturally, the more opportunity the employee has to earn premium, the greater will be his "take-home pay."

Operation	Standard	Pieces Done	Time Earned
Drill Complete	4.2 min. ×	145 =	609 min.
(less) Time taken (8 hours)			480 min.
(equals) Premium time			129 min.

Fig. 10-5. With wage incentive, everybody wants the earning opportunities of full days.

The time "on standard" is largely in your hands. You can exert control over the way time is spent. By more expertly running the department you supervise, you can greatly improve the showing you make.

Time Lost

It was in this phase of time lost that "piecework" was so unfair. Under piecework, the operator was paid for only what he did. That was before a minimum wage was guaranteed. Even with a minimum wage, often the employees' earnings were reduced because the "time lost" was not allowed. As you would know, the amount of lost time subtracts directly from the employee's earnings. You will see this on the chart in Figure 10-6.

Don't "Pad the Payroll"

Remember, however, the arithmetic you learned in the second grade. You are not being fair if you permit the "padding" of delay and off-standard time reported. By showing more off-standard time than actually occurs, you will unfairly increase

	Time Earned	
Time-card Record	Delays Reported	Delays Buried

120 Pieces × 5.0 Min. =
Time Worked 8 Hr.—   480 Min.
  (less) Delay   30 Min.
  (equals) Premium Time
	600
	
	450
	150
		600
		480
		
		120

Fig. 10-6. When credit for delay is not given, it comes out of premium earning.

the premium paid. Earnings will be inflated. The incentive earnings get out of line. Then you will really be in hot water.

Operator Interest

The employee on incentive is primarily interested in timestudy because it affects his earnings. His questions may seem to show otherwise. But that is only because he wants to know why his earnings are not something more. His "more money" is not always a result of the "gimme" attitude. Quite often, it is the desire to get ahead. It is expressed in dollars instead of responsibilities. Because incentive has a major effect upon his earning capacity, the employee is very definitely concerned. Keep in mind that roughly one-fifth of his income can be directly affected.

Explain Both Sides

Therefore, you must make it your business to help your people earn "real money." One easy way to help them is to do a good job of explaining timestudy and incentive. This means giving complete instructions about both sides of the bargain. First, make sure that each person knows what methods are to be used and how to use them expertly. Then, be certain that he understands exactly what kind of a job is to be done to produce the quality product your company sells. Further, do your utmost to see that every job is on standard so that he has a chance "to go to town." Besides, plan the work so that delays are small and see that full credit is given for those that occur. Finally, keep poor working conditions to a minimum. But insist that proper allowances are made for those that do exist.

Satisfying the Employee

The important job of understanding both sides of the incentive plan is greatly assisted by standard data. That is because of its consistency. Also, the conditions are standardized for a whole group of jobs. Consequently, the explanations of standards are not difficult. There are fewer details to question.

Besides assisting you to maintain standard conditions, data helps you to sell the standards being applied. Each time you satisfactorily explain a standard, the data is better understood. After this has been done often enough, the employee begins to feel that any standard correctly set from the same data will be fair also. More confidence is established. Then, the employee who turns out incentive performances earns substantial premiums. Earning more adds a lot to employee satisfaction.

CHAPTER ELEVEN

Explain Your Incentive Plan

"Our incentive plan is too complicated. I can't figure out how much I got coming."

Is that so or isn't it? Maybe you agree with the statement. My experience is different. Even those men with little schooling can tell you to the penny how much incentive pay they have earned. How they do it is more than I know because some incentive plans are very difficult to figure.

Getting Up-to-date

In the past, many incentive plans have been devised and used in industry. There are more than 25 named plans besides piecework and measured daywork. Fortunately, most of the complicated plans are no longer used. The modern ones are much simpler. Most of these plans are but variations of a few basic principles. They are easy to understand. And you should have a working knowledge of the general principles of incentive plans. You should know enough to be able to explain the details you will be asked about. These are easy to learn and you should know the general differences between plans.

Incentive plans are extremely helpful to successful operations. As Crawford Greenewalt says, "The importance of financial lure is . . . because money is the only form of incentive which is wholly negotiable, appealing to the widest range of seekers."

Basic Incentive

The principle of incentive appeals to practically everyone. For that reason, almost any wage incentive plan is better than daywork. Although the most powerful incentives are not financial, most people think of them in terms of dollars and cents. This is particularly true when incentive is mentioned in connection with timestudy.

But do not be misled. Too many people think that the main reason for timestudy is to set "rates." It isn't, of course. The main purpose is to *study time* to find where the leaks are and to stop them.

In the same general way, many believe that incentive is a cure-all in production. You may have heard men say, "Just wave a buck and you'll get production." That isn't true either. However, as just stated, incentive does appeal to most people. But remember, incentive applies to people. It has nothing to do with the type of industry or the kind of work. Further, it is true that most people will turn out more production for more pay. But, that is where too many men stop in their thinking.

Three Provisions

You can see why if you read carefully the next three statements.

1. Full gains in productivity require the supervisor to go to work also.
2. Reductions in lost time take your best efforts and planning.
3. Corrections in working conditions eat up much of your time and energy.

If your competitors are willing to skip the big gains from incentive, then maybe you can get the jump on them. You can use timestudy and incentive for their real purposes.

Hopefully up to this point, you have acquired a better understanding of timestudy. Now, let's discuss incentive plans. Later, we will tie the two together.

Incentive Fundamentals

First, we will take a look at the basic fundamentals that make up incentive plans. They are four in number.

1. Way of setting the basis.
2. Form of expressing standards.
3. Method of figuring earnings.
4. Share of earnings paid.

Timestudy versus "guesstimate." The incentive and method of computing extra earnings may be based upon sound timestudy standards or on "guesstimates."

Time versus dollars. The time values used may be stated as definite times per piece or as so much money per unit of output.

Individual versus group. The extra output may be paid for by giving full credit to the individual who did the work or by prorating the earnings over a group.

One-for-one versus sharing. Most plans pay all the over-standard earnings to those involved. But, some pay only part.

Piecework

From those basic variations, we can go now to specific plans. Descriptions of a few typical plans should give you all the general information you will want. The explanation might well start with an old-timer. Our oldest wage incentive plan is piecework. It is the one most people are familiar with. It is easily understood because it is like all retail trade. So many dollars or cents are paid for every operation that is satisfactorily completed. Piecework is now quite often based upon timestudy. However, in many cases, the prices are the results of compromises. As an incentive plan, piecework usually combines

"Guesstimated" allowances	Individual compensation
Dollar piece prices	One-for-one payments

Long ago, the employee could be paid for just what he produced. Then, it meant that an employee who produced a half day's work received only a half day's pay. There was no guaranteed minimum earning. The absence of a guarantee is sometimes cited as an advantage. The lazy employee gets paid only as much as he earns. That attitude may be alright in some instances.

But poor planning may keep the fellow from producing. He may not have the things he needs to go ahead and work. True, he would be paid for the work turned out. But he may have been ambitious and have wanted to earn more. This is an exceedingly important point that should be remembered by those who argue that piecework is the only system.

Disadvantages of Piecework

The attitude that the employee is paid for only what he does is the main objection to piecework. If management does not care whether or not people earn real money on incentive, then productivity is low. As a result

1. Average earnings are usually low.
2. Good producers are apt to leave.
3. Overhead costs are excessive.

Now, labor regulations require that a minimum wage be guaranteed. It is continually rising. Yet, in comparison with other plants in a community, the guarantee may still be low. It need not be but often is because of the attitude already mentioned.

Then there is another grave disadvantage. Piecework prices are stated in dollars even when they are based upon good timestudy. When time and money are combined, one of the problems of the foreman and the timestudy man is increased. This difficulty arises when the employee says that he cannot earn enough money. A "tight rate" may be caused by either a base rate or a standard that is low. But the complaints usually go to the timestudy man who deals only with time elements, whereas the base rate is the responsibility of management, beginning with the foreman. The jockeying back and forth often results in a "horse trading compromise."

In addition, piece rates have to be refigured each time there is a wage increase. Or total earnings must be factored. Or the piecework is paid on a sharing basis. Keep in mind also, management must run a duplicate system based on time if it wants to know individual performances, do a real job of production planning, and get correct product costing.

Halsey 50-50

The oldest named plan is Halsey. This plan is one that usually combines

Past performance records	Individual measurement
Time standards	Sharing payment

Many foremen are familiar with the Halsey premium plan. It was frequently used in the early days to introduce incentive without bothering to take timestudies. Past performance records were used and the plan usually paid the employee half of the time saved. However, because all kinds of inefficiencies were included, some jobs could be improved much more than others. The result was that earnings were highly irregular and too frequently excessive. Unfortunately, some companies made the mistake of "cutting rates," as implied in Figure 11-1. Thus began the "cut and try" methods that created so much criticism of timestudy and incentive. This often happens when companies do not want to make the effort to take correct timestudies. As a consequence, many employees still wonder if a guarantee of standards will mean anything if they really do try to make higher earnings.

Objections to Halsey

The chief objection to the Halsey plan is the use of past-recorded times. This is overcome in some plants by using timestudy. But then the procedure is to greatly increase the resulting times so as to use the sharing principle. That seems foolish,

Fig. 11-1. "Boss, last time I did this job they gave me 30 minutes."

even though the timestudies may separate most of the wasted time. The benefits of the sharing method do not offer enough advantage to offset the inflation introduced. As a matter of fact, the extra time added for sharing brings in an important disadvantage. It permits the payment of extra earnings starting at about 67 percent of a "fair day's work."

A study of Figure 11-2 brings out this point. The chart was based on 15-minute allowance given for a 10-minute standard time. If the job is done in less time, then half the time saved is paid to the operator. You can compare earnings on the Halsey plan with those on piecework on the curve in Figure 11-3.

Time Allowed	Time Taken	Time Paid for	Efficiency
15	12	13.5	83
15	10	12.5	100
15	8	11.5	125
15	6	10.5	167

Fig. 11-2. Observe under Halsey the relations between time taken and time paid for.

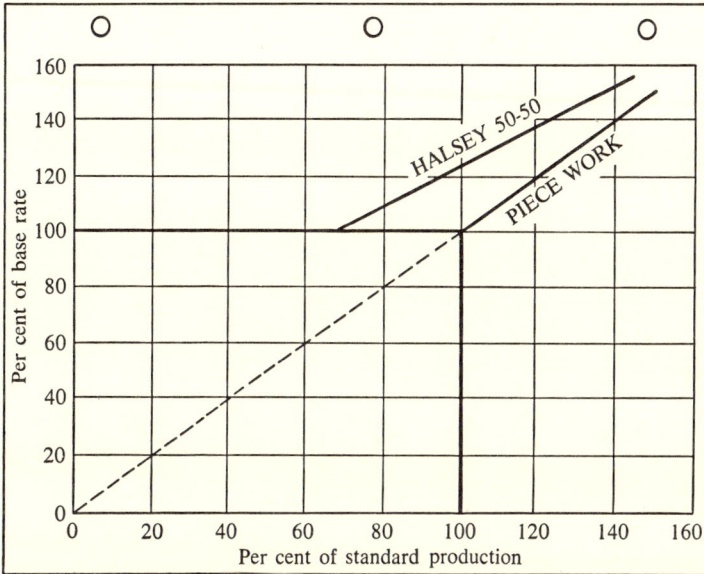

Fig. 11-3. Relation between earnings with Halsey and piecework plans. Line below 100 is dotted to indicate minimum wage guarantee.

Gantt Plan

Another of the basic incentive plans was developed by Henry L. Gantt. He originated a step bonus plan for those who attained the standards. His plan was designed to use a low base rate. This was to be increased substantially, in some cases 30 to 50 percent, for the attainment of the time standards. All production above 100 percent "efficiency" was paid for at the increased base rate. The plan combined

Timestudy basis	Individual payment
Standard times	Extra incentive

Today, a number of plants use a modified Gantt plan with a 10 to 12 percent jump in base rate at 100 percent performance. Everything over standard production is paid for at the higher rate.

Disadvantages of Step Bonus

The lower guaranteed base rate is a big problem when a company is trying to hire skilled men. The users of the plan are apt to find that, in reality, they pay the market rate or more as base rate. The result is that the jump in rate at 100 percent actually becomes a corresponding increase in cost. Observe the curve in Figure 11-4.

Some may argue that this is not an increase in cost because employees are not expected to attain high earnings. They may feel that the employees will average 115 percent instead of the usual 125 percent. Were this true, the labor cost per piece would be about the same as if a higher base rate were used and the step bonus eliminated.

Point Plans

Sometime after the Gantt and similar plans were devised, a number of "point" plans came into being. These combine several of the better principles previously described without carrying over too many of their disadvantages. The standards

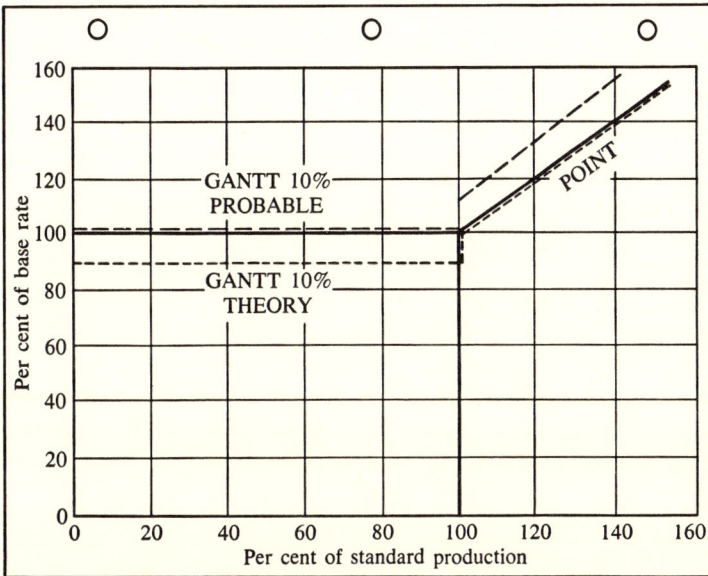

Fig. 11-4. Comparison of earnings under Gantt and point one-for-one plans.

are set in units, points, manits, norms, and Bs. All these terms are trade names meaning *one minute of good work*. The elements of these plans are

Timestudy basis   Individual payment
Standard times   One-for-one incentive

Some of the early point plans used a sharing basis. The portion not paid to the operators was for use as incentive to supervisors and indirect service people. Now probably, all pay 100 percent premium. Today, this is commonly called "one-for-one." These plans gain the feature of piecework by allowing so much time per piece instead of so much money. That method permits the continuation of the standard times through changes in the level of base wages.

The point plans are most apt to be used with a guaranteed wage rate equal to or slightly higher than the community rate. The production is then measured against the time taken to perform the work. The increase in earnings begins, as with piecework, when the standard has been attained.

Advantages and Disadvantages

The plans that use standard time units are as simple to compute and understand as piecework. They allow a standard time per piece or operation. The standard time multiplied by the pieces produced equals so many minutes earned. The excess of these over the time worked on incentive is the premium time. This extra time earned is changed to money at the job rate per minute. When this is the practice, the man's base rate can be the same or different. This flexibility is not available with piecework where the operator may be given lower grade work to do.

The point plans are the ones used in the more up-to-date plants. And the time standards set for them are more correctly established. Usually, the modern point plans pay separately for all delay time. In the better setups, no delays are buried in the standards. That means better average productivity. Delays are reduced when everybody sees how much they cost. Delays are too expensive when the base wages guaranteed are equal to community rates.

Group Payment

Some of the plans previously described may be applied to groups of people. While the group method of payment is often called the "group system," it is really not a system. It is a method of payment. It is usually based upon time standards but can operate like piecework with money allowances. The old form of "contract" is an example of a group payment on a piecework basis.

Commonly, a group standard is set by combining the standard times for the several operations performed. Quite often, the wait time of unbalanced operations and other extra costs are included. The output is calculated as the group standard multiplied by the number of good pieces produced. For example, suppose a three-man group, on a standard of 30.0 minutes, each working 8 hours, together produced 60 pieces.

If this were ordinary piecework having an hourly rate of $2.82, then the total payment would be $84.60 ($2.82 × 30/60 × 60 pcs.). Each man would get a third or $28.20 because their hours were equal. On the other hand, those using a time and "efficiency" basis would figure differently. They would compute the "efficiency" and multiply it by the hours worked and the individuals' base rates. Both sets of "earnings" are shown in the chart in Figure 11-5.

	Wage Rate		Hours Worked	Per Cent Efficient	Payments	
Name	Man	Job			Hr. Rate × Eff.	Piece Work
Jones	$3.10	$2.82	8 X 125		$31.00	$28.20
Smith	2.70	2.82	8 X 125		27.00	28.20
Brown	2.40	2.82	8 X 125		24.00	28.20
					82.00	

$$\frac{60 \text{ pieces} \times 30.0 \text{ mins.}}{24 \text{ hours} \times 60 \text{ mins.,}} = 125$$

$$60 \text{ pieces} \times \frac{30.0 \text{ mins.}}{60.0 \text{ mins.}} \times \$2.82 = \quad 84.60$$

Fig. 11-5. The amount paid to individuals in a group depends upon how you figure it.

Three Performances

The previous examples assume that each man did the same amount of work. Maybe they did. They may have helped each other. That is not likely in a progressive operation. So let's take a likely case of an unbalanced series with correct work standards and compute what each man did. The results are shown on the chart in Figure 11-6. There you find three more different amounts that can logically be computed.

1. Standard minutes produced multiplied by $.047 ($2.82/60 min.).
2. Individual wage rates multiplied by personal "efficiencies" for 8 hours.
3. Individual wage rates times 8 hours plus premium minutes earned times $.047.

The third one is the method I think is the fairest. We should pay the man his base rate for the skills he brings to the plant.

Name	Wage Rate		Std. Each	Std. × 60	Per-form %	Payments		
	Man	Job				Mins. @ $.047	Wage × Eff.	Wage × 8 Prem $.047
Jones	$3.10	$2.82	11.0	660	138	$31.02	$34.22	$33.26
Smith	2.70	2.82	10.2	612	128	28.76	27.65	27.80
Brown	2.40	2.82	8.8	528	110	24.82	21.12	21.46

$$\frac{\$2.82}{60 \text{ mins.}} = \$ .047 \text{ per min.}$$

Fig. 11-6. Knowing individual performances permits three other ways of computing pay.

His premium should be paid at the value of the work done.

Comments about Group

By the figures shown in charts in Figure 11-5 and 11-6, you can see that the usual methods of calculating group earnings do average the productivities of those who work in it. As a rule, neither the man nor the company has any measures of individual skills and abilities. See Figure 11-7.

It can be argued that incentive inequalities are taken care of by differences in base rates. That might be true if each individual worked at a pace comparable with his base rate. It might be so also if no one ever got a raise because he had been with the company for 10 years. But generally, the high producer shares his premium with those below the average in the

Fig. 11-7. Individual skill and ability are not measured and recognized in group incentives.

Fig. 11-8. "Mr. Jones, I'm tired of carrying those slowpokes on my back. I'm going where I can get paid for what I can turn out."

group. These higher skilled or more energetic men prefer to get paid for their own efforts. When they are not, they are apt to slow down to the average or go to some other plant. Notice Figure 11-8.

Measured Daywork

Still another incentive plan came into being before World War II. It was called Measured Daywork. Primarily, it was designed to smooth out incentive earnings. The measurement part of the plan was maintained to adjust the base rate up and down. The adjustment was based on the average performance of a prior period. The time intervals of the period varied. One month and three months were two periods frequently used.

These long intervals of time made it next to impossible for the employee to relate any increase in pay he got to his improvements in productivity. Consequently, the effects of incentive were largely lost. Further, the base rate was supposed to be reduced when the employee did not maintain the production that earned the increase. But it is questionable if this part of the formula was regularly carried out. It is especially distasteful to cut a man's base rate after he has had it for three months.

Current Term

Nowadays, people use the term "measured daywork" to mean something entirely different. Today, men say "measured daywork" when they mean work measurement. Standards are set. Performance is measured. But no money incentive is paid for above standard output. As a result, few people perform above standard. The losses are two. First, the men have no opportunities to earn about 25 percent more money. Second, the company loses the capacity increase, delivery improvement, inventory turnover, and fringe benefits.

Indirect Labor Incentive

All the advantages of incentive apply equally well to the indirect employees. Indirect people should be given the same opportunities to increase their earnings. They want to enjoy the higher standard of living as suggested by Figure 11-9. Therefore, incentive opportunities should be provided. Otherwise, wage rates are likely to be increased to pay for "lost opportunity."

But, any form of proportional payments is the wrong approach. The work should be measured. Direct standards

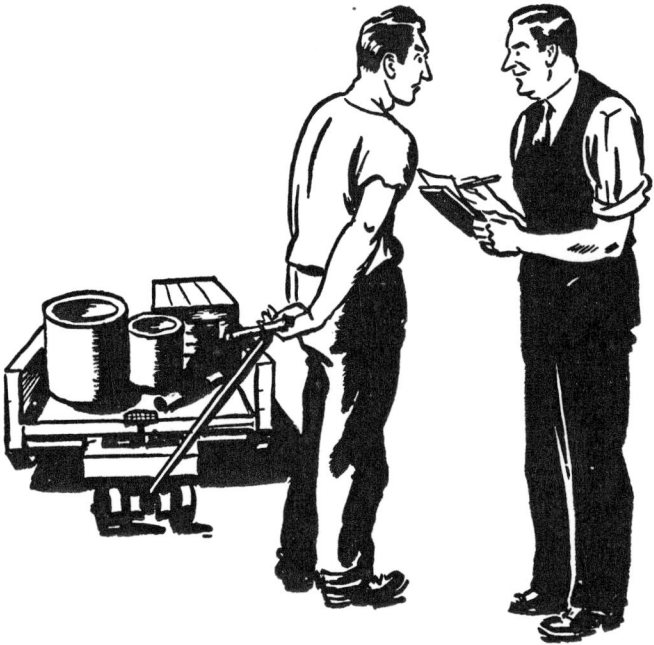

Fig. 11-9. "Chief, why don't I get a chance to earn some extra money like the operators do?"

should be set to measure office, toolroom, janitor, maintenance, setup, repair, and similar types of work usually classed as overhead. Direct standards have been applied even to much of the work done in engineering departments. Operations treated as overhead by many foundries, namely, casting, cleaning, pouring, and shakeout are usually measured by direct standards when the timestudy men have been properly trained. Such applications of incentive to indirect and overhead operations produce increases in earnings and outputs.

Normally, you are held responsibile for the control of the expense of your indirect people. You are expected to operate within your budget. In doing so, you would be greatly assisted by having time standards set so that these people could be paid incentive.

General Considerations

Many of the variations in incentive plans that have been described were worked out to accomplish certain results. Many of the desired features are advantages only under specified conditions. Practically speaking, all these plans should be compared in terms of the final results. That point is the expected average incentive production. This average production might have to net the same earnings if the firms using the several plans were competitors in the same labor market. With operators moving freely from one plant to another, it is assumed that the "take-home" would have to be the same for like amounts of production.

However, competition for business and labor has not been severe enough to bring incentive plans closer together. Actual differences do exist. Some companies pay more wages than others for the same production. Yet, regardless of "take-home pay," certain companies have much lower unit costs than the average. They get better performances with their people, and they make use of better methods. Keep in mind, it is not what you pay that determines labor cost. It is what you get for what you pay—productivity.

CHAPTER TWELVE

You Can Improve Methods

"No, you can't do that. We tried it once before. It won't work." How many times have you heard that or a similar statement? Very often is my guess.

Can't Be Done

One explanation is that many people react from habit. Often they hide behind the statement, "That's not common sense." Be careful you don't fall into the same trap as suggested by Figure 12-1. Common sense told people it was impossible to fly, impossible to talk over wires, impossible to see things hundreds of miles away. Remember, common sense told people that the earth was flat. Yet, we are going around the world with our airplanes, telephones, and televisions. We have even landed men on the moon.

Fig. 12-1. Avoid thinking you are the only one who has good ideas.

Recall the story about the Wright Brothers. Even though they had made a successful flight in a heavier-than-air machine in December 1903, scientists, newspaper editors, and our War Department would not believe it for nearly four years. But the flight was successful, as you well know. Think where we would be today if we didn't have planes. However, the proof that something was done changed the attitude of only those exposed to the facts.

Better Operations

Facts that are helpful to you are brought out by timestudy. Hence, your progress and that of your department is just beginning when work measurement is installed. A momentum is set up that calls for further improvements. This is fortunate for you for two reasons. First, men who get ahead are those who "make things happen." Second, every plant must make improvements to continue to be successful. The company must hold its position competitively or no one will have a job.

The gains that can be made are of three basic types:

1. Reductions in waiting time within and between jobs.
2. Corrections of conditions that cause extra work.
3. Improvements in methods that reduce work required.

Reduce Interferences

Developing better methods may be more interesting to you. But I believe it is the mark of good supervision to first get your department working more effectively with your existing methods. Two reasons stand out. One is that reducing interferences can be done without spending money. The other is improving morale. People prefer to work without interruptions.

Waiting Time

The easiest interruption for you to reduce is waiting time. Much of this occurs between jobs. Hence, you should plan ahead. Try to have everything ready before jobs start.

Then, you may have some concealed waiting. One place to look for it is in unbalanced work loads. The unbalance is quite noticeable in some assembly operations. It is not so apparent, however, where work is done by a group or in a line. Frequently, the leader is the "bottleneck" of the operation. He holds up the efforts of all his helpers. Such a condition should be seen by the timestudy man. Nevertheless, observe carefully every operation that involves two or more people. Often, major savings can be made by doing a better job of balancing the work loads.

Process Waiting

Then, there is another kind of waiting you may have. If yours is a machining department, look critically at your operations. You may find instances where the producer works while the machine is idle and he is idle while the machine is operating. This condition deserves your attention for several reasons. In the first place, you should understand that "machine wait" is relaxation time the manual workman does not have. For example, the foundry molder works full time. In contrast, the machine operator may apply his skills only half the time. Secondly, the work-wait cycle does not have the rhythm that people prefer in their work cycles. Thirdly, the waiting is costly.

Consequently, it is fair to arrange machining operations so that the producer has work to do during the "wait time." This is common practice in many trades. It becomes increasingly important that you utilize some parts of the machine time as you move further toward "automation."

Added Operations

Another fruitful source of savings is in eliminating added operations. Usually, these operations were started to overcome some defect. They are created as emergency measures. But such operations have an unhappy way of staying with us. Because "we have always done it that way" may suggest it is time to make some changes. Commonly, these operations are added to correct defective workmanship. The defects may have been passed along by the previous department, the foundry, or the vendor. Note: Good workmanship has already been paid for. Therefore, the added operation is added cost. The work is being paid for twice.

Operations of this kind can be eliminated entirely. Persistency may be necessary. Not so much of this will be required if you get the facts. The proof is often fairly simple. Often, you can get the information you need from the timestudy man. Such improvements are very pleasing because, in many instances, they can be made at no cost except those of discussion.

Extra Finishes

A different type of "added operation" occurs when the finish of the product is more exacting than commercial tolerances require. True, everyone likes to see a nice-looking product. That is perfectly normal. But the commercial side must be considered. This applies particularly when the extra fine finishes are not seen by the public.

Being out of sight is not to be confused with "having a dirty neck." Frequently, fine finish merely adds to the appearance of the product. It does not improve its functioning. And, if the part cannot be seen, there is no reason for the fine finish. Therefore, take a second look at your finishes if you have such operations. Repeatedly, better definitions of requirements have resulted in big savings.

Unnecessary Exercise

Then there is another kind of unnecessary effort. For instance, in one plant some stands were made for an assembly operation. These were built to raise the work up to bench height. They were made of concrete because the work was heavy. But, the stands were made the same size as the assembly. No extra space was provided for either tools or parts. Hence, every time the producer needed a tool or the next part to be assembled, he had to bend over to pick it up off the floor.

Bending is very tiring. And yet, every day we waste effort in unnecessary bending and reaching. Look at the benches in your department. Are the parts to be worked with arranged in nice neat rows at the very backs of the benches? This reminds me of a question someone asked, "Why not make the benches wider so the parts can be placed farther away?" Such everyday examples are amusing. They give the impression of having been designed to waste energy.

These extra efforts should be converted into extra pieces by reducing the bending and reaching. The station where the operator works should be arranged with a view to saving effort. The unnecessary exercise should be changed into useful work by shortening the distances. Eliminate the calisthenics. The producer will be less tired at the end of the day, and he will have turned out much more production.

Job Analysis

When some of your general losses have been cut down, you should look at the operations themselves. A simple approach to job study is shown in the table in Figure 12-2. This notes four classes of the producer's time. You should study it carefully. It gives you an easy way to break down any job so as to see possible improvements. The *productive* part is all that really counts in turning out good pieces. Yet, the producer is spending lots of time on the other three kinds of elements. Handling is an accepted part of his work. But it can be reduced by improvements. Indirect and lost time may be done by someone else so that the producer can apply his skills more often. Also, recognize the opportunities to improve machine utilization.

Productive

Mill Keyway
Clean Casting
Turn and Bore
Inspect Thread
Make Mould

Handling

Tighten Vise
Piece Aside
Chuck Piece
Gauge Aside
Place Flask

Indirect

Change Cutter
Move Material
Grind Tool
Remove Burr
Bend Wires

Lost

Oil Line Broke
Power Off
Wait for Gauge
Wait for Print
Wait for Sand

Fig. 12-2. You can divide the elements into four classes to help you find improvements.

Individual Jobs

You can improve upon many job details. These gains will increase your production and lower your costs. Generally, the
leaks you find will come from working on one job at a time.
You may make a change to eliminate one type of loss equaling
as little as 1 percent of the time worked. Yet, if your idea has
general application, the total turned into useful production
might equal 480 minutes (480 × 5 days × 1.0% × 20 men) per
week. You must not be discouraged when you save 20 percent
on one job, for example, and the total reduction for the week
is only 480 minutes. Working on one job at a time is a long
process. Even so, the improvements are well worthwhile when
the changes are recorded and the standard times are reduced
accordingly. Then, when the jobs are repeated, the improvements are actually put to use.

Pieces per Hour

The kinds of improvements you can make in machine and
equipment costs are so important, I want to emphasize them
by an example. Let us examine a common drill press operation. A simplified timestudy might show the sequence recorded on the chart in Figure 12-3. There you can see the total
time per piece of 1.23 minutes. The standard of production is
about 49 pieces per hour. But notice. The drill time of .42
minute is the only true *production* element in the cycle. It is
only 34 percent of the whole time per piece. That tells us we
could get 143 pieces per hour at standard if we could do drilling without all the "put and take."

The machine utilization would improve greatly and so
would your costs if we could reduce the "makeready." Maybe
Figure 12-4 will emphasize the point. You can see in the

Element	Minutes		Per Piece
Wait For You.......	15.00	15/250	.06
Grind Tool.........	10.00	10/100	.10
Pick Up Piece.......	.05		.05
Place In Jig.........	.12		.12
Oil Drill............	.04		.04
Locate..............	.03		.03
Drill...............	.42		.42
Remove Piece.......	.09		.09
Blow Chips.........	.05		.05
Inspect.............	.11		.11
Aside..............	.04		.04
Hunt Tote Box......	20.00	20/250	.08
Wait Material.......	10.00	10/250	.04
			1.23

Fig. 12-3. Element analysis of a drill press operation.

IT'S THE "MAKE READY"
THAT TAKES THE TIME!

Fig. 12-4. Much productive time is lost during the make ready. (Drawn by Guy Rutter for Woods and Gordon, Toronto)

diagram in Figure 12-5 how each added element reduces the pieces per hour and the machine utilization. Study this diagram. Observe that the elements have been arranged in order of decreasing necessity. From this example you may learn ways

Element Added	Elements in Order of Necessity	Accrued Time	Pieces per Hour	Machine Eff.
	Drill...............	.42	143	100
1	Pick Up........... .05	.51	118	82
2	Aside.............. .04			
3	Place In Jig........ .12	.72	83	58
4	Remove Piece...... .09			
5	Blow Chips........ .05	.77	78	55
6	Inspect............ .11	.88	68	48
7	Locate............. .03	.91	66	46
8	Oil Drill........... .04	.95	63	44
9	Tool Grind......... .10	1.05	57	40
10	Hunt Tote Box..... .08	1.13	53	37
11	Wait Material...... .04	1.17	51	36
12	Wait For You...... .06	1.23	49	34

Fig. 12-5. Note in the right-hand column how each added element reduces the machine utilization.

to improve the output of your equipment. Probably, you can eliminate or reduce elements that cut into the productivities of your people and of your equipment.

Two Fixtures

Now, here is a similar idea you should consider if you have machining operations. This approach helps considerably to cut costs and to increase capacity. But this one will cost you money. Observe in Figure 12-6 a man-machine combination. It is simplified to show in the upper half a cycle consisting of about 50 percent handling and 50 percent machining.

Suppose you have quantities to run. Then, you should consider getting a second jig. With it, you would achieve a result like that shown in the lower part of Figure 12-6. Both the man and the machine work more hours during the day. Do not assume, however, that the problem of balancing man and

MACHINE-MAN TIME DIAGRAM

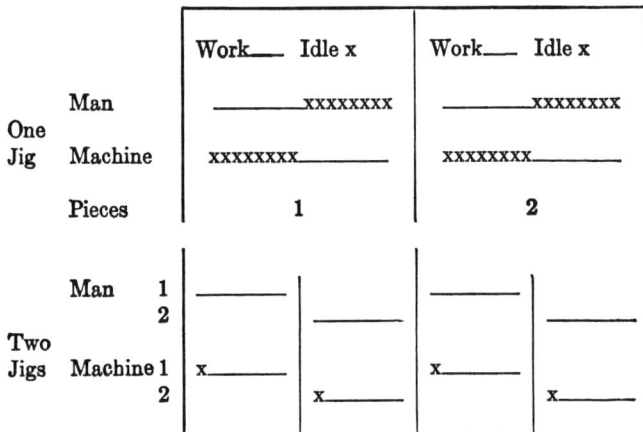

Fig. 12-6. Observe how two fixtures may give you both better man and machine performance.

machine time is always quite as simple. Regardless, the saving in machine time often makes a greater change in total cost than could be brought about if all the labor were eliminated. That is because the machine usually costs much more per hour than the man. Machine time saving is very important when you consider *total cost*.

Presenting Suggestions

Going back to the subject of two fixtures, getting approval to spend money takes skill. You must learn how to interest your boss in new ideas. Having the necessary persuasive skill is very necessary to the foreman who understands timestudy. That is because timestudy is one of the most fruitful ways for developing suggestions for improvement.

Some will require okays on requisitions for tools, jigs, or fixtures. Maybe you will need money to pay for a rearrangement of the department. Whatever the suggestion, you can get facts from timestudy that will help to determine the gains to be made. These can be compared with the costs to make the changes and used to help your boss make the decisions. Also, your training in timestudy will assist you in selling the good ideas developed in your department.

Bill's Millstone

Fortunately, some boss-men are anxious to get better methods. To illustrate, here is a story about a foreman named Bill. He certainly knew the work in the shop. He could do it and could teach his men to do it. He knew his work so well that he could find dozens of reasons why a new way would not work. He had balked at most things new many times before I met him. To him, timestudy was just one more new idea.

Some time later it was decided that Bill should be given timestudy training. Four months after he had started, the vice president went to him with some questions about a new process. He was nearly floored when he discovered that Bill no longer offered his usual objections. Instead, Bill asked for some time to dig out the answers. Next day, he told the vice president what he wanted to know. Then, he suggested that the new method be tried and gave his reasons why. This pleased the boss very much because he was greatly interested in developing new methods. Bill has since been made a plant manager. His change in attitude toward progressive ideas removed the millstone that was holding him down.

Be Open-minded

Many of us prefer to avoid tangling with the boss. Yet, he is always pushing for "cost reduction." Therefore, changes have to be made. In that direction, almost everyone in the organization thinks about better ways of doing things. The timestudy man especially is trained to look for better methods. He asks the advice of any and all who can help him solve a given problem. It is a part of his regular duty to receive and to make suggestions for method improvements. Are you going to help? Will you be on the lookout for better methods? Will you grasp the opportunities to show this kind of betterment in your costs? Will you get the timestudy man to help you put across the good ideas you have thought about for years?

Are You Receptive?

Yes, I know, sometimes the resistance to change comes from above. To illustrate, the foreman and his chief were out in the plant looking at some spoiled work. The freshly printed pattern had been smeared. This happened because the man controlling the tension in the long strip of linoleum had "fallen asleep" for a minute. The piece had been dragged against the edge of the drying shelf above it.

After some thought, the foreman said, "You know, Chief, I think an electrical contact could be made to automatically control the tension." Quickly the boss said, "You're crazy, that won't work." That reply "took the wind out of his sails." But the foreman went ahead. He had one made and installed. It proved to be okay. Then he asked his chief to come out to see it work. When the boss saw how nicely the new gadget controlled the tension, he was very pleased. Turning to the foreman, he said, "That's fine, Joe. Go buy yourself a good cigar."

Even though the superintendent did say, "It won't work," he was quick to praise the foreman when he saw the result. But the average foreman might not have had the courage to go ahead. He could have let the good idea die a natural death. This could have been easier than taking a chance on the boss' negative reaction to being proven wrong.

Do It Yourself

Of course, there are many ideas you can carry out with little help from anyone. However, you should think carefully about the overall effect. Remember that old saying, "If you want a job done right, do it yourself." That may be correct for some particular job. But, it is not correct from the standpoint of good organization. What you really want is teamwork. Everyone must be taught to do his job properly in a well-run organization.

Doing something for the other fellow does not give him the training he needs, as you see in Figure 12-7. Nor does it permit you to do your job. Letting him do his own work incorrectly and smoothing out the difficulties afterward does not solve the problem either. Consequently, you should be striving all the

Fig. 12-7. Do you believe the saying, "If you want a job done right, do it yourself"?

time to get your people to suggest better ways. Everyone has the creative instinct. Men and foremen alike feel the urge to suggest very strongly.

Interest Your Men

Both say, "There must be a better way." The questions are, "Can you work it out?" and "Will it pay off?" Chances are you can say "Yes" to both questions with the help of your men. They have ideas, too. Some are darn good ones. But there is an angle that is more important. Your men will become more concerned with the success of "their" department when you can put their ideas to work. Remember, all of us like to see our own ideas carried out. Only the chances for advancement and for steady work are more important to us.

To get ideas, you must be receptive to the suggestions of your men. Otherwise, you have to "go it alone." Your attitude can drive away the help that others can give you. "Give" is the right word to use. Withholding is the easier choice if you resist. Thus, when suggestions come from your men, it is doubly important for you to listen.

Your Men Have Ideas

Your men are trying to "get ahead" also. Making suggestions for improvement is one method of showing that they have some interest in the future of the company. Its future has a vital bearing on theirs. Consequently, you must honestly try to find the good points in the ideas advanced by others, your own men in particular. By discussing with the suggestors all new ideas brought out, some good is almost certain to result. Discussion sets to work the imagination and ingenuity of the two people concerned. One advances an idea and the other, in an attempt to agree or disagree constructively, usually brings forth still further improvement.

Recall how frequently we see ways to improve a jig or fixture as soon as it is completed. To reduce the number of such proposed corrections and also to help make suggestions more practical, you should encourage your men to discuss their ideas with you. Discussion can be particularly helpful when the shop has a regular suggestion plan. The reasons are

1. To help the producer make his suggestion workable.
2. To encourage the employee to make known his ideas.

Withholding Suggestions

Even in plants where good suggestion systems are working, ideas for improving methods are sometimes not turned in. Notice Figure 12-8. Let me relate a "furinstance." A man about

Fig. 12-8. Most men have ideas and want to suggest them, but they expect the proper recognition.

to be pensioned visited the works manager to reveal three splendid ideas he had used for years. He had been on incentive for more than ten years and had used these shortcuts most of that time. He was to be complimented for explaining his methods before he left. Nevertheless, his company and his supervisor had failed to sell him the soundness of the suggestion plan. For a long time he had been paid for work he did not do.

Sell the Suggestion Plan

Take another case. A foreman knew that one of his men used a trick gadget for assembly work. He wanted to make several of these tools so that all his assemblers could use them. Yet, he felt that he could not do so in fairness to the inventor. At the same time, he failed to persuade the man to turn in his suggestion. And so time went on and production was lost.

1. The man was paid daily for work he did not do.
2. The incentive earnings were way out of line.
3. The standard time was incorrect for the job.
4. The increased production by others was lost.
5. The operation sheet did not show the method used.
6. The new man could not be trained in the better way.

The story can be told only because the foreman knew about the improvement. But the point is that the man was not sold on the suggestion plan. Besides, he might have left the company and taken his idea with him. In this instance, there is not more than one chance in 100 that he could have used his idea in another plant. Therefore, it is stressed that the foreman has a job to do. He must make every effort to have his men offer their suggestions to him or through regular channels.

They have many. These should be paid for according to their values. Then everybody can use the better methods and the costs will come down. The standard times can be made correct and so can the operation sheets.

Giving Credit

Suggestions from employees should be reviewed promptly and utilized whenever they are economically sound. Their values can be determined from time facts obtained from timestudies of the operations being changed. The advantages of the suggestions can be calculated from the time elements affected. These can be compared with the costs to make the changes. The net gains or losses will then be known. Sometimes, a suggestion is not practical because the production quantities are too small.

With figures, suggestions can be presented on the basis of facts. Action can be taken quickly and correctly. Both are important from the standpoint of making understandable explanations to the suggestors. You can explain with confidence when you have the "figures." With facts, you would certainly give full credit to those who made suggestions. This principle of good leadership cannot be too strongly emphasized.

Resistance to Change

Learning how to make changes is a necessary part of timestudy training. The timestudy man recognizes that all of his work has to do with changing things. He knows also that it is normal for most people to resist changes. To succeed, he must learn how to get along with people and to accomplish all the other tasks assigned to him.

Training in the proper approach to making changes is likewise helpful to you. You must know how to introduce changes to those who work with you and also to your superiors. You are well on the road to succeeding in this effort when you yourself have forgotten "Can't be done" and learned to say instead "Let's try it."

CHAPTER THIRTEEN

How Your Job Changes

"Where am I going to get foremen like those in the A. B. Company? It takes twice as good a foreman as any I have to run a department using incentive," so Mr. Gould, the vice president, said when he decided to put in an incentive plan. Perhaps he was exaggerating. However, there is no question about the big difference in skill required.

Direction of Pressure

One thing that changes noticeably is the direction of pressure. On daywork, the foreman has to keep after his men to get out production and to reduce costs. On incentive, the reverse is true. His men push the foreman to

1. Keep them supplied with plenty of work.
2. Reduce all the delays and lost times.
3. Get the machines and their tools fixed.

4. Furnish materials in good condition.
5. Have proper time standards set promptly.
6. Give better instructions and training.

Planning Work

The one word "planning" describes most of the advancements you must make in your supervision. You must learn to think ahead when your men are on incentive. You should have everything ready so they can work. The reason is quite clear. Extra earnings to the tune of 25 percent are at stake. This premium is reduced when things go wrong. You must offset trouble by better planning.

Delay Time

Planning will help you to reduce waiting time. This is necessary because under good incentive plans, waiting time is paid for separately at the base rate. Waiting time is not buried in the time standards. That makes the control of this lost time one of your major problems. You can reduce the amounts of waiting by correcting the causes:

1. The boss (you) does not have the next job ready.
2. The inspector is too busy to check the first piece.
3. The setup man has not prepared the machine.
4. The tool crib man is running shorthanded today.
5. The timekeeper is trying to check his figures.
6. The trucker has not yet delivered the material.
7. The men responsible have not done their jobs.

In these many ways, extra earnings are lost while waiting. For example, assume that a man can earn two extra hours pay on incentive. You can expect about 25 percent added earnings under the usual incentive plan. That is the same as one-quarter hour or 15 minutes extra per hour on incentive. Hence, each 10-minute delay reduces the incentive opportunity. The man might earn only one extra hour if he waited for half a day in small amounts like 10- and 15-minute delays.

Delays Buried

While attempting to reduce the wait time, you must make certain that all you do have is reported. You need the reports in order to study the reasons why waiting occurred. Besides, if all waiting time is not reported, your men will suffer losses of premium. The arithmetic showing how this happens is given in Figure 13-1. These are the same figures you saw in Chapter 10.

The example is computed both ways. It is easy to see how failure to report the 30-minute delay actually costs the producer 30 premium minutes. In other words, he pays for the delay out of his own pocket.

Time-card Record		Time Earned	
		Delays Reported	Delays Buried
120 Pieces × 5.0 Min. =		600	600
Time Worked 8 Hr.—	480 Min.		480
(less) Delay	30 Min.	450	
(equals) Premium Time		150	120

Fig. 13-1. People on incentive should be given credit for delays.

Incentive Opportunity

You just saw how delay time reduces premium earning opportunity. The same applies when jobs are run without standards. And so you must make every effort to get standards set for all your operations.

You must assist your men to get maximum opportunities to work on incentive. You will get help from the timestudy man who wants to get standards set for all jobs. He knows that the employee's opportunities to earn premium are dependent upon having standards set. Therefore, he wants to keep daywork at a minimum. But he needs your help. You must tell him when some of your jobs lack standards. He can't be in two places at once. Therefore, you should give ample notice. Otherwise, the busy timestudy man may be forced to choose the jobs he will set. Being only human, he may choose to work with the foreman who helps him the most.

You must recognize that you and the timestudy man are working toward the same goal. There is no escape. Your men will go after full incentive opportunities whether or not you work with the timestudy man. That is bad for your department. You want teamwork. And so, you have to be a good captain in order to attain that goal.

Follow-up

You recognize, of course, that planning is only the starter. Planning will turn out to be "castles in the air" if action does not follow thinking. It is not enough to assume that

1. Previous departments will get work in on time.
2. Maintenance will fix the machines promptly.
3. Timestudy will set standards as they are needed.

Too many supervisors think that their jobs end when they issue instructions or notify the other fellow who is responsible. "I told him" is not enough to prevent delays. Telling him may not avoid the loss of premium earnings of your men. That's where the pressure starts. That's why the foreman of an incentive department has to be a better supervisor.

That's why after planning, you must follow up. You must "carry on." Right here is where so many men lose out. Most of us can start. But very few finish what they start. This factor of *follow-up* makes the biggest difference I know between successful men and the garden variety. And so keep going.

Knowing Your Job

Follow-up is necessary especially with all the jobs that are on standard. Here again is one of the big problems. Since most of us are lazy, we assume when we have set up proper conditions that they will stay that way. Not so. Things will slip. This involves you in two ways:

> *First,* you must know exactly the conditions that determine the standards.
> *Second,* you must see that they exist each and every time the job is run.

Faulty Conditions

Completely understanding the details of the jobs in your department is very important. These show what the working conditions are supposed to be. Conditions must be maintained reasonably uniform. The reason is that good timestudy standards do not include broad averages of variable conditions.

Obviously, when working conditions get out of line, the men may lose premium.

If the stock is too heavy or the material too hard when operations are on daywork, the extra time taken causes no hardship for the producer. However, when premium is involved, you hear about these difficulties promptly. Then you must take steps to remedy the conditions or else see that proper time allowances are made. This is one reason why knowledge of the way standards are set is so helpful to you. You can use it most effectively toward maintaining the normal conditions.

That effort is aided by the ability to readily detect faulty conditions that have not been corrected. Getting extra time allowances promptly is possible when you are on the alert. Remember, however, faulty conditions may continue to occur until you run them down to their sources.

Correcting Conditions

Poor working conditions can make time standards appear to be badly in error. Also, they make it evident that the foreman does not know what is going on in his department. This comes out when he hollers "tight standard" and a check study later shows that something has slipped. Maybe the variation occurred since last he saw the operation. But had he investigated, he would have phoned the Timestudy Department, as shown in Figure 13-2, that

> *"The stock on this lot is excessive. Will you come down to see what the extra time should be?"*

> instead of

> *"The standard is too tight!! Can't any of you timestudy men ever get the right answer!!"*

Fig. 13-2. Make sure you know what you're talking about when you call the Timestudy Department.

Keep in mind that the conditions of material, tooling, instruction, method, and other controlling elements *do change*. Some change with progress. Most variations are the results of slippage. They may not be your fault at all. Still, you are the supervisor, and you should see that conditions are made right.

Avoid Losing Production

It is clear to you that after conditions have changed, the standard no longer applies. The working conditions must be brought back to normal. Or an allowance must be made. The standard and the conditions must be related. If you take the easy way out:

1. Standards will change frequently.
2. Wastes are buried in time allowed.
3. Production falls off considerably.
4. Costs keep on rising skyward.

Faulty Workmanship

You may have to do extra work because the job was not completed on previous operations. The incomplete work may have been done by an outside supplier or a previous department. One of the most common illustrations of faulty workmanship is found in assembly work. Often, assemblers are required to fit and file parts that should have been completed on the machines. Usually you find that the mechanic was paid to complete his operation so that parts would go together in assembly. The mechanic may have been careless about removing the burrs or holding his tolerances. Occasionally, of course, you find that he did his work exactly to specifications that were in error. In either event, some extra operation is required.

Double Payment

Under such circumstances, the "rework operation" is a second payment for that part of the job. If it were your money, you would not pay twice for something. You should feel the same way about paying extra for work to make a job right.

At this point, you are faced with a choice between two problems. They conflict. You can be fair in work measurement only when the man is allowed time for what he has to do. But the extra time allowed because of faulty conditions raises your costs and reduces your production. Then the boss is after you.

Are you going to pay extra for added work by having high

costs? Are you going to keep on losing production by doing extra work? When you do, your men must be allowed for the necessary added work. But that time is wasted. Why not cure both headaches by seeing to it that the work is done correctly in the first place. A permanent cure is the best answer. That is what you would seek when you are on incentive also.

The Other Side

Not all abuses of wage incentive reduce the employee's earnings. Some cause inflation. Those should be understood also. They come about through failures to maintain the correctness of standards. You can help in many ways to see that the fairness of incentive earning opportunities is maintained. You want to avoid all the headaches that arise from inconsistent standards. You want to be sure that earnings are correctly related to good work done.

Excess Earnings

Excess earnings can result from poor timestudies. Usually, however, high earnings are brought on by padding the records and by failure to keep the standards consistent with the methods being used.

Changes in methods are taking place all the time. The wide-awake foreman knows that the methods and conditions in his department are changing, mostly for the better. That is part of progress. No one should wish to stop or delay the making of improvements. Advancements are necessary to the raising of our standard of living. But, before such betterments can truly raise our standard of living, they must be reflected in reductions in cost. Obviously, there is no reduction in cost when the timestudy standards remain the same after the methods have been improved.

Tight and Loose Standards

Failure to notify the Timestudy Department of improvements makes the foreman a party to "inflation." Unfortunately, there is likely to be much more of this inflation in some jobs than in others. The possibilities are greater. This unevenness makes for inconsistency in earning opportunities. It creates the situation of "good and bad jobs." Averaging the good with the bad will not solve any problems. Letting some men pick out all the good ones will make the situation even worse.

Some foremen kick to the timestudy man when they think the standard is wrong. That is what they should do. But, most of their kicks have to do with "tight" standards. Many of the tight ones appear that way only because they are compared with loose ones.

Most of the loose ones are caused by method changes that were not reported at the time they were introduced. The result is that higher premiums can be earned for the same effort. The jobs are easier to do because part of the work has been eliminated.

Top Limits

Some of these variations are like the changing of the oil in your car. There is no definite check on whether it was done. Many times, and in many ways, you can get away with phony things that substantially raise the earnings of your men. That is why it is so necessary for you to understand timestudy. You should know what can happen so that you can play the game according to the rules.

When we try to get something for nothing, we usually lose out in the long run. In wage incentive, that often comes about when we pay for work that is not done. Earnings climb. Then somebody yells, "The men are earning too much." That is a false statement. They are not "earning" too much. They are being paid too much in unearned premiums.

High "take-home," when it is earned, is very desirable from my point of view. But overpayment for *work not done* cannot be solved by setting limits on earnings. Setting top limits is perhaps the worst thing that can happen. It destroys incentive. In so doing, it hurts everyone. You may rave and rant when such a thing happens, but you may be largely to blame.

Correcting Standards

Setting a top limit is to work on effect, not cause. It is a remedy, not a cure, as suggested by Figure 13-3. Certainly, consistency must be maintained or the incentive plan becomes unfair to some employees. To avoid this unfairness, the stand-

Fig. 13-3. "Top limits" serve only to stop production when the man has earned his "day's pay."

ards must be changed when methods are improved. These changes must be made at the time the better methods are started. It will not do to say, "It is only a minor change, let it go." Continuing the old standard through a very few minor changes will make it loose. It will be unfair by comparison with other jobs. Then the problems multiply. I'm sure you can see the advantages of avoiding this kind of trouble.

Little Changes

Keep in mind that minor changes do add up. That is critical because you are so apt to be on the lookout for only the big ones. In your opinion, a 10 percent change may be big. Yet, five changes of 2 percent each equal the same amount. Besides, 2 percent is not small. Isn't that just about half what you make on your government bonds?

The problems growing out of "minor changes" can give you very painful headaches. You can avoid them just as you can escape the "next morning headache." The answer is, "Don't get in so deep." You will save yourself a lot of trouble when you notify the Timestudy Department of all changes. That means you must call attention to the improvements and short-cuts. You cannot be a foreman who "hollers" only when he wants more time and still expect to have a smoothly running department.

Fall Down

All the factors discussed here affect the man's performance and his pocketbook. Any injustice suffered will bring on poor in-dustrial relations. This may cause indifference. The producers may say that you can't get any place around here. They may coast along and not even try to make premium. This is aggravated when loose and tight "rates" are part of the working conditions. You may have your hands full then. You can't be sure whether the man "falls down" because he does not try or because he has not learned how. One is a much bigger problem than the other.

Lying down on the job can be overcome by changing the man's attitude to one that looks ahead. Inefficient performance can be corrected by training, instruction, and encouragement.

Performance Record

The loss of some premium earnings is only part of the story. The man's performance record has to be considered also. It drops down when his earnings fall. To some men, this is more important than the money loss. Personnel experts say that the desire to get ahead is more vital to many people than the amount of wage. Both factors are injected into your responsibilities when your men are on incentive.

Man's Status

The man's performance record ordinarily shows his "efficiency" and spoilage. These figures tell the quantity and quality of his output. Of course, these factors are by no means the only considerations of importance in a man's value. They are, however, the big ones in many jobs. They are the only ones that are easily measured. For that reason, they carry a lot of weight when layoffs and promotions are made. Either change in a man's status is certainly important to him. It is more vital than the small amount of money lost by failure to report waiting time. Therefore, you must keep in mind the man's performance record. Furthermore, you must make the effort to help each of your men maintain a good showing.

Improving Skill

The performance record measures only what the producer actually does. It does not show what he might do on his present or a higher grade job. But the pressure for promotion forces you to give your men chances to work on better jobs. That is true also on daywork. But the point here is that with incentive and timestudy

1. There is a record to show how well a man performs on more difficult work.
2. There is available an easy way of training producers to do specific jobs.

The training is made easier by the use of timestudy details. These enable you to instruct employees to do jobs correctly in standard time or less. The timestudies show (1) the necessary elements of work and (2) the proper sequence of elements. By using written information, you can train consistently and the producer learns more quickly.

Then you have the added advantage of closely observing the men's progress. As a result, you know more exactly the aptitudes each has. This knowledge helps you to guide each man into the work he is best fitted to do. The result is that the performance record will show how much the man is improving. That is of real value to the man who is trying to get ahead.

The urge to progress is strong in each one of us. You will develop this urge if you really want to be a good foreman. In this direction, the work performance records will be of great assistance to you. Naturally, you will progress also. You must in order to stay on top of a department that hums.

CHAPTER FOURTEEN

Are You Looking Ahead?

"What good does it do me to learn all about timestudy? That's something for the timestudy man to worry about," you say. Well, you can look at the subject that way. Many do. But you can't get very far in your present job with that attitude. Let me try to explain why to you.

Suppose the president of your company went around the shop taking timestudies. You would become very interested in finding out why he was studying time. For the same reason, you interest yourself when the boss asks about the cost or the delivery of a particular job. In reverse, whenever you can get your boss concerned about something you want to do, it takes on more importance in your mind. That attitude toward our superiors is the result of our childhood training. We have always thought that whatever our parents or teachers did was alright.

Know Your Stuff

In the same way, your men look up to you because of your personal skill in your trade. Similarly, they would respect your knowledge if you were skilled in timestudy. With such skill, you could add a great deal to their understanding of any discussion of timestudy you might have with your men. Also, your attitude toward timestudy, cost reduction, and methods improvements would be reflected by your people. Consequently, their performances and thus the showing of your department would be better. And let me go on to give you some more reasons that are vital to you personally.

Are You Forgotten?

To begin with, you may have read in articles and books that the foreman has been neglected. He was forgotten alright. But whose fault was that? He can say that management should have trained him better. There is no denying that much could have been done to improve supervisory training. However, the man who thinks enough of himself to want to be promoted should look to his own education in management subjects. He wants to be management's representative. If he hopes to be a good one, he may have to *prepare himself* to hold his position.

Self-improvement

Management can give you the job and the title, with or without training. But you have to hold it. That is especially true if you were one of those supervisors who were shoved ahead because of early retirements. Many such foremen had no previous training. Ever since, many have been too busy getting out production. Many were not trained for the new conditions brought in by unionism. Sadly, many can't be bothered with developing themselves. They may wonder why they are demoted later if production falls off. They should be giving serious thought to ensuring their own upward progress. More training and more study are necessary.

What Makes a Foreman?

First off, you are selfishly interested in getting along with your immediate boss and management in general. Too, you must be able to manage the people in your own department. You can make progress in both directions when you do your own job better than average and can make yourself well-liked and respected. To be "management's representative" in the shop, you must have management's point of view. Perhaps, you have not been trained to think like a manager. Under these conditions we may hear it said that the company "spoiled a good workman by making him foreman."

Logically, most foremen are selected from the working group. However, giving a man the title "Foreman" and perhaps an increase in wages does not make him a foreman. He has to be trained to think like a manager. In this training, my belief is that he has to learn to think first of profits and company security. That is his only way to preserve jobs for himself and his people. In this respect, knowledge of timestudy can be most helpful. In my opinion, timestudy work is the best training ground in industry.

Peculiarly, many supervisors think that timestudy is used only for setting work standards. That is an incorrect assumption. It has many more important applications. Perhaps, in a particular plant, there are no other uses made of timestudy. That may be because questions about processing, layout, capacity, and similar problems have been pretty well answered. Then again, it may be that the Timestudy Department has not been used to get facts as fully as it could be. Regardless of the reasons, you must remember that timestudy is not and should not be used only for setting standard times. Yet, you need to thoroughly understand this use for setting work standards because all the other advantages grow out of this one.

Representing Management

From your position, the first fact you should learn from time-study is the necessity for sticking to the "middle of the road." Both the workman and the company must get full value. You must be equally fair to producer and to your management. Training in this understanding can be very helpful to you. It greatly assists you to keep your personal feelings out of your day-to-day decisions.

Further, timestudy training should enable you to see more clearly the relation between wages paid and product turned

Fig. 14-1. Ambitious foremen understand costs and can explain them to their people.

out. Learning to think in dollars should help you to explain the company viewpoint more clearly to your group. You can point out much more definitely the necessity for making profit in order that employment continue. Notice Figure 14-1.

Certainly, you can get this view of business operations without having been a timestudy man. But you may have to dig it out for yourself. It is not likely you would get it while acting as an assistant foreman. It is easier to get it through good training in timestudy. That gives you the cost-profit understanding. Sound training would make this relation of cost-profit a permanent part of your thinking process.

Putting Ideas Across

In discussing cost, too many foremen are apt to consider only labor cost. Are you one who does? Take for example, the question of making some method improvement. One should figure the cost to make the change *before* it is authorized. That cost would include expenses that become a part of overhead. But the savings should not include any labor overhead. That usually goes on just the same. Probably, the overhead rate would go up following the reduction in labor. And many companies expect that the savings will pay for the cost of the change in one year.

Profitable Changes

Understanding this relation between labor savings and the costs to gain them is of concern to you. You may find it better to forego making certain "improvements" because you cannot afford the expense. You will be satisfied to drop unprofitable changes. Training in this way of thinking would make your requests for auxiliary tools less frequent. But they would be more emphatic. Those would be justified by factual information.

Hence, you would escape the worries of those foremen who think their bosses have it in for them when their ideas are not adopted. You will know what you are talking about when you start in to sell an idea. And you'll admit that knowing "how to sell" is a skill you can use anyplace in your future.

You would have to learn "selling" if you worked in the Timestudy Department. You would find that you must use different methods to sell ideas to different people. As a timestudy man, you would have to succeed in selling time standards and methods improvements. You would be forced to learn how to use various approaches if one fails to accomplish the result you seek.

Part of an Organization

What has been said about timestudy applies to many other subjects. The knowledge gained from time spent in study makes you less of an expert. The more you study, the more you find out how little you really do know. This is not said in any slighting way. It simply means that the more anyone inquires into the fields of management, the more he realizes how much there is to be learned. The good timestudy man recognizes this. He sees the connections between work done in one department and the functioning of the whole organization when he discusses the solutions to his problems with other department heads.

The timestudy man is required to work with practically all departments. He has discussions with production, accounting, planning, engineering, inspection, and sales that broaden him. These people teach him many reasons why things are done as they are. He acquires a much better picture of the relationships between all the elements of cost. More knowledge of the

Fig. 14-2. Foremen and timestudy men can learn a great deal about management from other departments in the organization.

departments named would assist you to do a better job. It would give you a keener sense of organization. Observe Figure 14-2. It would guide you in recognizing how your work fits into the company operations as a whole.

Releasing the Brakes

As you look around and study what you see, the wheels begin to turn. Then if you take on some knowledge of these other company functions, you begin to look ahead. "What's next?" you may ask yourself.

To move up, you must seek training in the subjects you must know in order to do the next higher job well. Besides, you must train a successor. You will not only do a better job of selecting and training him because of your broadened viewpoint. But also you will do it early and thoroughly. In your training, you will know that old-time trade secrets are common knowledge to those who take timestudies. Besides, seeing how silly it is to guard your job, you will be much more concerned about progressing beyond your present position than hanging on to it.

You cannot train others for promotion without realizing that you must stay ahead of them. You don't want to get run over. At the same time, you will know that you can get ahead only with the help of your men.

Being More Flexible

To make progress, of course, you must get into the habit of changing. I don't mean just to keep things stirred up. I'm talking about finding better ways to do things. Think of all the development and research that goes on in manufacturing concerns today. Better ways for making our present and future products are being devised every day. The makers of equipment used in turning out our basic products are striving to sell their improvements to us. As these are adopted and put into practice, the standard times for your operations must be reduced. Otherwise, the money invested in new equipment does not fully pay off.

We Must Progress

Reductions in time allowances are sure to result from the changes we can all expect. It is inevitable that methods and processes will be improved. That may be why one works manager I know objects to the term "standard" when applied to time allowances. He says, "The word standard assumes something fixed." He goes so far as to say that the time allowance should be lower on each successive run because improvements have been made in the meantime.

It is possible to use the word standard and still make progress. Yet many of us are inclined to think that a standard is more permanent than it should be. For that reason, you want to work for progressive changes. Don't buck them. Don't try to stop progress. Instead, help yourself to grow by aiding your company in turning out better products at lower costs.

Controlling Costs

In understanding costs, timestudy training can assist you. Like most of us, you need to know more about what makes up overhead cost. You should learn why it goes up when method improvements are introduced. Knowledge of cost is necessary to your success. It enables you to grasp the relation between work done and dollars spent. With that knowledge, you can do a better job of managing your department. In addition, you can more readily comprehend the problems your boss must contend with.

You should be able to see that until you really know what costs are, you can hardly expect to move up to the boss' job. A working knowledge of the purposes and methods of cost-keeping is another thing you can get from training in timestudy. With that understanding, you will realize that management is not doing its job properly unless it asks you to explain your high costs. Further, you will have discovered that you do not have to wait until you are asked *why* before you prepare to answer those questions. You know, of course, that it is easier for you to get your answers while the facts are fresh in your mind. Thus from training in getting facts, you would make your own job easier and your work more constructive.

Foreman Premium

Going further with cost control, many plants provide incentive for supervisors. The better plans reward men like you according to how well they control costs. Such plans have standards for the payroll costs of salable production. Then, as the foreman reduces actual costs by lowering losses due to waiting time, indirect labor, and scrap, he makes more premium. Other factors are measured too. But here I have tried to point out why you should interest yourself in controlling your time costs—and also why you can put to profitable use a thorough awareness of how to study time.

Make Your Own Opportunities

Timestudy is the best means we have today for measuring the productivities of people. But production is not limited to turning out pieces. Productive efforts are by no means confined to the shop. Production is also done in the office, in the Maintenance Department, in the Engineering Department, and in the Inspection Department.

For a working knowledge of all these other functions, you should be interested in becoming an expert timestudy man. When trained, you will realize that your worth to your company is dependent almost entirely upon the contributions you make towards its progress. Your attitude will become one of attempting to increase your worth. You would measure your personal accomplishments just as you would measure productivity in your own department.

Facts Remove Prejudice

Finally, training in timestudy helps you learn how to get the facts. That training is extremely useful in your striving to get ahead. Being trained to use facts instead of opinions makes you less apt to be prejudiced in your judgments. You are able to see the disadvantages as well as the advantages. You can render decisions that are made more nearly obvious because of the facts. That in itself will do a great deal toward advancing your position in your organization. Getting the facts will help you also in presenting ideas to your boss. Your boss wants the answers instead of the questions. But your answers must be correct.

It's Up to You

Now, you know all about timestudy, I hope. What are you going to do with your newly acquired knowledge? Are you planning to use it to help you turn out better products at lower costs? If so, you can start using the *study of time* to improve the operations of your own department.

Some men have taken full advantage of their timestudy training and made real progress. Some have attained top jobs in their companies, as suggested by Figure 14-3. Would you like to get up there too? "Sure," you say. Okay, let's go to work.

Fig. 14-3. Timestudy training has helped many a good man to promotion.

Begin to apply what you have learned. Plug up the cost leaks in your operations so that they stay fixed. Try to make your department and your company the best in the industry. Then nothing can hold you back. More power to you.

Timestudy Aids Management Training

1. A supervisor who has had sound timestudy training will see more clearly the relation between the wages paid and the products turned out.
2. A supervisor who knows timestudy can make a much more clear and complete explanation of work measurement to his people.
3. A supervisor who utilizes timestudy details can more easily train his people to correctly turn out quality products.
4. A supervisor learns through timestudy how to analyze ideas more correctly, assemble facts, and present them to his superior.
5. A supervisor with an understanding of timestudy will balance the cost to make improvements against the savings before advocating changes in methods.
6. A supervisor trained to analyze will anticipate and record sound explanations of increases in his costs and losses in production.
7. A supervisor learns from timestudy a great deal about the proper function of his department as a part of the whole organization.
8. A supervisor trained in timestudy will have a much better understanding of the work done by Production, Accounting, Planning, Engineering, Inspection, and Sales Departments.
9. A supervisor trained to think in terms of cost can more easily and clearly explain the company's point of view to his men.

10. A supervisor who gains the loyalty and respect of his men will be given the chance to adjust their complaints before they go over his head.
11. A supervisor who knows how to analyze will insist upon having up-to-date reports that correctly show the amount of progress he is making.
12. A supervisor bent on "getting ahead" realizes that he cannot make progress without the support and help of his own people and he takes every opportunity to build them up so that they can push him ahead.

INDEX

Index